Let your positive energy flow & look for the laughter! Meg

From the Stage to the Page
- Life Lessons From Four Funny Ladies

Judy Suke,   Meg Soper,   Judy Croon,   Susan Stewart

i

From the Stage to the Page
- Life Lessons From Four Funny Ladies

Copyright © 2011
Judy Suke, Meg Soper, Judy Croon, and Susan Stewart

Printed in Canada 2011

ISBN 978-0-9866578-0-1

Publisher: Triangle Seminars
Mississauga, Ontario, Canada

Printer: Ball Media BOOK FACTORY, Brantford, Ontario, Canada

Cover Design by Vickie Fu and Dennis Bartel

Judy Suke Cartoon by Willem Pretorius
Judy Croon Cartoon by Ileana Grimm
Susan Stewart Cartoon by Marybeth MacLean

Four Funny Ladies came together to bring you this book.
We dedicate it to our family and friends;
the people who nurtured our humour
and put up with us through the years.

We also dedicate it to our readers
with heartfelt wishes
that it bring you joy in your life.

Table of Contents

PART I

By Judy Suke

About the Author:

Judy Suke is a Motivational Humourist, College Professor, Corporate Trainer and Author. She has a reputation for being informative, entertaining and memorable. She held management positions in the corporate world and has served in executive positions on various volunteer boards. Throughout the years Judy has earned many awards  of achievement and certificates of appreciation, including: The Apprenticeship Board's "Employer of the Year"; Mississauga "Woman of the Year", for volunteer efforts; the Ontario Government's Certificate for "Excellence in Human Resources"; the "Pinnacle Business Woman of Distinction" for excellence in education and training, Distinguished Toastmaster Award, District 60 Toastmaster of the Year, for leadership; and she won both the Toastmaster District 60 Humorous Speech Contest and the Stand-up Comedy Contest in Niagara Falls. A member of the Canadian Association of Professional Speakers, she is the Past-President of the Hamilton Chapter.

Judy is the President of Triangle Seminars where she has a terrific team of trainers, speakers and entertainers. A popular speaker at conferences and corporate events, Judy's mission statement is – to bring humour and hope to people around the world.

www.triangleseminars.com

INTRODUCTION

I personally believe that in order to survive in this hectic world, you have to have a sense of humour. I also believe it is easy to have a sense of humour. I realize that some of you may have to work *really hard* at it. Especially, if you are not accustomed to letting yourself enjoy life. But, the effort is worth it.

Because, I think a sense of humour is so important, and laughing is what you need to do, I am willing to share some of my most embarrassing experiences, and crazy ideas with you. It is my hope that they will not only set a good example for you, but, they will also entertain you, make you laugh out loud, and provide you with some tips to help you get through life.

I dedicate my section of the book to my mother, Helen Hamilton, who always showed me, through her constant example, that life is much easier when you have a sense of humour. Also, thank you to my sisters, my children, my friends, and my husband, who have done things that provided material for me.

Now, sit back, relax and allow yourself to laugh and enjoy the book.

"We all have moments in our lives that test our courage. Taking children into a house with a white carpet is one of them." – Erma Bombeck

Judy Suke

Chapter 1
Let Laughter Lighten the Load

When we put our minds to it, we can train our subconscious to react to situations with humour. We just have to work at it for a while, until it becomes a habit. You can start by reading books that laugh at life's little trials and tribulations. Read this book, and more books by Judy Suke and such authors as *Erma Bombeck, Bill Cosby, and Loretta La Roche.* Through the words of other people you can learn to *Let Laughter Lighten the Load.*

> **Buy and read humorous books to lighten the load of stress.**

Humour, It Works For Me

I can honestly say that I am a happy person. Other people, who know me, would say so too. They might add the word crazy. That's all right. It helps to be a little crazy when dealing with what life throws our way. When there is a lot of incoming 'crap' to deal with, the ability to laugh at it, and see the funny side of events, can definitely help you to get through it.

Although, I have been divorced; survived two heart attacks and four mild strokes; suffer from the pain of fibromyalgia and arthritis; have become 'full-figured', and can no longer work in a regular job, I thank God every day for my wonderful life. I know firsthand, that laughter has the power to heal the body, soothe the soul, lift your spirits and give you energy.

The Healing Power of Laughter

Over the last couple of decades, even the medical profession admit that laughter has healing power. Tests have shown that a good laugh, lowers blood pressure, exercises the lungs, and raises the level of oxygen in the blood. It also releases endorphins, the body's natural painkillers, and these can relieve pain for several hours.

You may be familiar with the story of Norman Cousins from his book *'The Anatomy of an Illness'*. Cousins had been diagnosed as terminally ill, and he was hospitalized with a debilitating disease of the nervous system. He decided that he would never get well in a place full of sick people, so he checked himself out and went to stay at a hotel across the street. That way his doctor could still keep an eye on him. There at the hotel, he had his friends bring him videotapes of the *Three Stooges,* the *Marx Brothers, Jerry Lewis and Dean Martin,* and other comedy greats. He found that laughing for 10 solid minutes, relieved the pain for several hours, so he could sleep. Here is the amazing part – he fully recovered from his illness, and lived another 20 years. He credits visualization and laughter for his recovery.

> **Watch funny movies with the people you love and experience the healing power of laughter together.**

Judy Suke

Do you feel overwhelmed by even your daily chores? Do you feel stressed? Then, heed my words. Come with me to *'the light side'*, the fun side of life. Learn to use your sense of humour. As you read through this book, I want you to let yourself laugh out loud. Even if you are in a restaurant, on a subway or on a bench in the park, ignore the people around you and laugh as hard as you can. They will be jealous. (Please make sure that you don't cover the title of the book with your hands because I want them to buy it too. Share the joy with others.)

No matter how bad things are, laughter makes you feel better. When you let yourself laugh, really laugh, like a child laughs, with uninhibited joy, you feel totally healthy, exhilarated, and empowered. When you are exhilarated and empowered, you can accomplish anything you want, you can overcome anything the world hands you, and you will rise above adversity. Even more important, once you adopt a philosophy of humour, you will **bring your spirit to life,** and the glow it creates will awaken your creativity, and will act as a magnet to draw goodness to you. People will want to be around you.

There will be many times in your life, when you will feel weighed down, and struggle to continue. Those are the times when it is most important to remember that *a sense of humour can lighten the load.* Be a good example for your friends, your fellow employees, and your children. Leave a legacy of laughter.

I love who I am and I love who I am becoming. I don't fight life, I accept it. I treat it like an adventure. And I keep notes when disasters or embarrassing things happen so that I can share them with others. (For this reason friends and family really worry when they see me writing notes.) Use the following simple tips and you will have more joy in every minute of every day.

Always Have a Sense of Humour

Jim Unger, the creator of the comic strip Herman says, "The key to happiness and freedom is a sense of humour. And a sense of humour is nothing more or less than the ability to laugh at our self."

A story from my life - I was working as a Human Resources Manager. I really wanted to be a stand-up comedienne and a professional speaker; big stretch. I was doing little gigs, speaking to the Lions Club, the Rotary Club, and women's Church groups and at small association events. Then finally, I was hired by the International Association of Design Engineers. There were Architects, General Contractors and Land Lawyers; an audience of 250 men (that is a whole other fantasy). I arrived at the hotel and for the very first time, they pinned a lapel mic on me. I thought I was so professional. I had a lapel Microphone, a big stage, and they were paying me well. As a Toastmaster, I was confident, I was poised, and I was flying. Two hours into the presentation, I called for a break. I went off to the washroom. As I came out of the washroom, people were walking towards me saying, "You really should turn that thing off when you go to the bathroom."

Off! I didn't know that there was an Off Button. The man had pinned the battery pack on my skirt, behind my back, under my jacket. He never said there was an Off Button. As I stood there in the hallway, with them waiting in the ballroom, I figured that I had three choices: # 1 - I could go home; which was tempting, but they hadn't paid me yet. # 2 - I could go in and ignore what just happened. What man in his right mind would tell me what he just heard? Or # 3 - I could make fun of it. So I entered the room, took to the stage and said, "Well, now that I'm relieved and ready to start, how about you?" Because I shared the embarrassing moment with them, I had them in the palm of my hand for the rest of the day. I also booked a large number of events from that one. I am sure that it was because I was willing to laugh at myself.

Life is like that. Share your funny stories, your embarrassing moments and your laughter with others and they will want to cooperate with you, and be around you.

Live In the Present
I saw a Ziggy cartoon that said, "There is no future, spending the present, worrying about the past."

Unfortunately, people tend to carry the bad memories from the past, around in an imaginary sack, slung over their shoulder, getting heavier and heavier, as they go through life ... (That is why old people are stooped over.)

People refuse to let go of the bad memories. This creates a ton of stress, weighing them down, and squashing the joy out of their lives.

Women are worse at this than men. Never mind the fancy computers. Women are born with a brain chip; a list keeper. When they yell at their husband, it is never just about what he did today; they will tell him every bad thing he did from the day they met, and some women can probably list off the dates he did them on.

Here is a story I heard that might help you stop carrying the past around:

A visitor to a mental institute noticed a frail man on the first floor. The man was wandering aimlessly, and was sadly repeating the name ... "Lucy, Lucy, Lucy."

"What is his story?" the visitor asked the doctor.

"Oh, that is poor Henry. Twenty-five years ago he was jilted on his Wedding Day by Lucy, and he has been here with us ever since."

They moved on. On the third floor, where the most violent patients were kept; where there was a code lock on the door, bars on the windows, and Straight jackets on the patients, the visitor's attention was drawn to a man who was smashing his head against the wall and shouting, "Lucy, Lucy, Lucy !"

What is his story?" the visitor asked.

"Oh. That's the poor man who did marry Lucy."

Just imagine the wonderful life Henry could have had, if he knew how lucky he was not to have married Lucy, and if

Judy Suke

he had just forgotten about her, let her go, and moved on with his life.

It is my humble opinion that we all have a Lucy; someone who hurt our feelings, failed us in some way, said the wrong thing, or didn't do what they promised. And we carry that memory around with us. It doesn't only affect the way we treat them, it affects the way we react to others. We see someone who looks like them, we're suspicious. We meet someone with the same name, we're suspicious. We get into the same situation, we're suspicious. It didn't go well last time. There is no way it will go well this time. We have to stop doing that. Just let it go and move on. Don't waste your energy holding on to hurt, resentment or anger. You look really miserable with these thoughts in your head and they cause sickness and wrinkles.

Control Negative Thoughts
They will hit you. We all get them. I believe the Dalai Lama and the Pope have negative thoughts. These thoughts can start first thing in the morning. "Why get out of bed?" "I don't feel well." "I have nothing exciting to do." "I can't do it." "Who am I to think this will work." "Everybody is mean." You need to start your day in a powerful way. Stand in front of your full-length mirror, totally naked, and say. "Aren't I amazing? I am alive and everything works. Today is going to be a great day." Then go out and have a great day. (Get dressed first. The police arrest naked people and you don't want to know why I know that.) I bought one of those new alarm clocks that wake you up to nice music. I put pictures of my grandchildren beside the

11

clock, so that I want to open my eyes. I bought a fancy coffee machine that you set the timer and wake up to the smell of fresh coffee. I just pretend that there is a good looking man in the kitchen making it for me. I dress in colourful clothes and play uplifting music in the car. I choose to set a positive mood in the morning.

Create *joyful thoughts* to replace the negative. When something great is happening in your life, capture the memory using all of your senses. See it, hear it, touch it, taste it, feel it. I was down at the beach with my two-year-old granddaughter. I was pushing her on the swing. I had bare feet walking in the warm sand; the sun was setting and the sky was beautiful; the wind was blowing our hair; the waves were crashing on the shore; and she started to giggle. It was that wonderful rippling sound of a child totally delighted with the world. I thought, "Life doesn't get better than this." So, I closed my eyes and created a joyful memory chip in my mind. Now if life gets painful, I go to the beach in my mind.

If your attitude towards life is negative then you will experience a negative world. You have to **choose to be happy.** Abraham Lincoln said, "People are about as happy as they make up their mind to be." Make up your mind to be happy.

My story: When I was 50 I moved back in with my Mom. She didn't see that coming. I had to drive for two hours to work in the morning and two hours home at night. One morning, I arranged an interview at 7:00 a.m. As a Human

Resources Manager, I was trying to 'steal' someone from another company. I drove to the office and when I reached across to the passenger seat, my purse wasn't there. The keys to the office were in the purse. No one else was going to show up until 8:30 a.m. plus, my day timer was in the purse. I had no choice, I had to go home and get it. I put a note on the door, apologizing and suggesting we reschedule the meeting. Then I opened my sun roof, turned on my music and decided that God just wanted me to listen to four more hours of music that morning. Then I allowed myself to enjoy the drive. I arrived at the office later that morning and said to the receptionist, "You won't believe the stupid thing I did this morning." I explained and we both laughed. I called up all of the missed appointments and did the same thing and we all laughed and no one was upset. Where some people would have been frustrated or upset, I chose to laugh.

My Mom is really good at this. I came to pick her up one hot August day. I had the sunroof open and left the car sitting in the sun. When we got in, the leather seats were extremely hot. I started to apologize and said that the air conditioner would kick in shortly. She smiled, leaned back into the seat, and said, "Oh, we can just enjoy the hot massage." Now, every time I get in, I enjoy the hot massage.

Don't Be Normal

In her book, *Life is Not a Stress Rehearsal"* Loretta La Roche says, "People who don't feel pressure to

Choose to be happy. Enjoy the hot massage.

conform to societal standards live longer happier lives." In other words, if you are not worried about people judging you, if you don't worry about what people are thinking, you will live a longer, happier life. Look for the quirky people in your life. They are usually easy to spot. They wear bright colours, they laugh a lot, and they live life to the fullest. Quirky people bring richness to the world; they are the inventors and innovators, once you find them, join them.

I've noticed that many people in their quest for self-improvement, in their efforts to be 'normal' become so dreadfully serious and stressed out that they lose sight of what's important in life. I think three things are important: connecting with people; finding pleasure in everyday things, and having fun.

To connect with others, get out of the house. When someone asks you to join them to do something, anything for that matter, take advantage of the opportunity. Don't let silly excuses hold you back. – It's raining. It's snowing. My back aches. I'm tired. I'm having a bad hair day. – None of them are valid.

To find pleasure in everyday things, learn to savour the moment. When I had my fourth stroke, I was too weak to stand at the sink and wash my face. So, I got the washcloth steaming hot, like you see in the movies at those fancy spas. I went and sat on the edge of my bed and washed my face. As I plastered the cloth on my face and slowly moved it around, I thought, "Boy, this feels so good." For fifty-six years I have been missing out on this.

Now, even though I am strong and well, when I wash my face, I get the cloth really warm and sit on the edge of the bed and savour those moments. When I hug my Mom, I close my eyes and really feel the hug and hold on to that moment. I go through the drive-thru at Tim Horton's and order an extra-large French-Vanilla Cappuccino. Then, I drive along savouring every sweet sip and thinking how lucky I am to live in a country where I can do that.

To have fun, try some of those things you did as a child. When was the last time you were on a swing? It makes you feel young and alive. If your bum is small enough, go down the slide. Choose the tube slides. No one sees you until you pop out the bottom and scare the heck out of the little children and the other adults. One of my favourite commercials is the one where the naked couple is jumping over the fence with their wine bottle because they have been skinny dipping at the neighbours. I think even if you have your own pool, you should skinny dip at the neighbours, it is just more exciting. At my age and size, it is no longer skinny dipping, it is chunky dunking. Have themed dinner parties. When people get to wear a costume, even an Hawaiian lei, they act differently, as if they have been given permission to have fun. Do things that give you and others permission to have fun.

Every morning I say a mantra that sums up these lessons. I want you to say it every morning too...

Live, Let live, Love and Laugh a Lot

"No one is listening until you make a mistake."
- Jane Seabrook, Author, 'Furry Logic'

Judy Suke

Chapter 2

Smile in the Face of Adversity, Embarrassment, and Stupidity

My mother always said, "God never gives you more than you can handle." **Sometimes, I think he pushes it.**

I have learned from personal experience; no matter how smart you are, no matter how educated you are, no matter how rich you are, no matter how organized you are, there will still be trials and tribulations, disappointments and disasters, illnesses and accidents, and overwhelmingly embarrassing moments in your life. As we strive for success, these problems and heartaches could weigh us down. Life is like that. It is supposed to be challenging.

These situations may be caused by adverse circumstances, other people, or even our own stupidity. The cause is not important. It is our reaction, how we deal with them that is important. Instead of focusing on bad things that are happening, we need to focus on what we want to happen next. Then we can let go of them and get on with our lives.

That wonderful Canadian comedian, Ed Broadfoot says, *"Humour is tragedy, separated by space and time."* I am suggesting that you tighten up the gap, and laugh while things are happening. It will truly help you get through it.

Here is a personal story; my experience on a trip when I was travelling from San Francisco to Toronto. I often share this story on stage in my keynote, *"Let Laughter Lighten the Load"* and a portion of the story was in the book, *"Expert Women Who Speak … Speak Out, Volume 3"*

After a high-speed taxi ride, up and down the hills of the city, being thrown from one side of the cab to the other, I was not in a good mood and felt sick. I may have had a slight hangover from the night before, singing at a Jazz piano bar, but it was definitely the poor driving skills that were aggravating my system.

He screeched to a halt, and just as I was getting out, jerked the car forward as he released the clutch. I practically fell out the door and chipped off two fingernails trying to catch myself.

I seemed to be the only one in the airport. With no one to direct me, and only poorly planned signs to guide me, I finally found my gate, and patiently stood there for 30 minutes. I examined my ticket again. It clearly stated that I should be there at 7:00 a.m. It was now, 7:30 a.m.

The airline clerk slowly sauntered up, swivelling her mighty hips in that Marilyn Monroe-type way. If anyone else had been there, she would have certainly knocked them over, as she swayed from side to side. Good grief, she was barely able to move in her tight little, extremely short skirt. The buttons on her tailored blouse were just about popping open, straining against a rather voluptuous chest.

Judy Suke

She was one of those annoying ... perky people. Shaking her curly blond hair, she smiled broadly, (no pun intended) and said, "Good mornin' Ma-am. Mahy I hepp ya'all?"

I squinted through my eyes and said, "Yah. I'm here to check in." Why else would I be standing there at that hour of the morning? She took my ticket, and typed slowly away at her shiny terminal, being ever so careful not to break her long, bright red nails. "Oh, dear may. We seemed to haff overbooked tha fliiiight. There is no seat fur ya'all, Mrs. Suck." Bad news, but she was still smiling, as if this was extremely humorous. This did not impress me.

"The name is Suke, pronounced like Luke." I said. "What are "we" going to do about it?"

"Oh! Jist haff a seat. Wi'll tack care of it fur ya'all." Her southern drawl was grating on my nerves. I dutifully took a seat. Two hours and fifty-five minutes later, she finally waved me forward. "The good news i-is, we can git ya'all home todah Mrs. Suck!" She actually sang this out with great pride. Her sing-song voice was just a bit too cheerful for me. Especially under the circumstances, and I would really have liked to pull her tight little blond curls. However, I had seen that horrible prison in the middle of the bay and did not want to spend any time there.

"The name is Suke, pronounced like puke." I reminded her. Mistakenly, thinking that because I used the word puke,

she would get it, and remember it this time. "What is the bad news?" I asked.

"Wellll. Ya'all are goin' ta haff ta tack three different planes to git thar. But, the last one will fly ya'all, all the whaey from Vancouver ta Torana."

Not exactly a direct route, I thought. However, I am a fairly cooperative person, so I said, "OK. Let's get these bags checked." I honestly believe that I even gave her an encouraging smile. Well maybe my memory isn't clear on that. But, let's say that I did.

She actually laughed. "So sor-ry," she sang. "Ya'all are flyin' with three se-e-eparate airlines. Ya'all will haff ta tack that luggage with ya."

I had been there three weeks. I want you to picture this: I picked up my oversized, over-the-shoulder garment bag and put it on my left shoulder. In my left hand, I grabbed my larger-than-life duffel bag (the kind that looks like you have a body in it). I then placed my big, old, heavy carry-on bag over my right shoulder, along with my ridiculously large purse; that happened to be filled with books, because I am a nervous flyer and wanted to read the whole way, for peace and tranquility. (Trust me. There would be none of that today.) With my right hand, I was just able to grab the leash of my suitcase on wheels. Not the nice new ones. It was one of those old rectangular ones with four wheels. One wheel was wobbly. (I believe they purposely sold them all that way, just to laugh at us while we struggled with them.) You would pull it ten feet and it would fall over. You would pick it up and pull it another ten feet, and it would fall over.

At this point, I was regretting my decision to bring everything I owned, in case of rainy, cold, hot, and dry or whatever weather conditions there might be in San Francisco in March. I also had a Chinese rice-patty hat that I bought for my children to add to the costume box at home. With nowhere else to put it, I wore it. It was one of those flat, wide-brimmed, (about two feet across) weaved grass hats. I knew I looked ridiculous, but what else could I do? Armed and ready, I gamely asked, "Which gate do I go to?"

She laughed again, really hard this time. Loudly enough, that everyone was staring at us. On the verge of falling over, holding hers sides, she finally blurted out, "Oh, dear may, Mrs. Suck. You aren't even in tha riiiight terminal. This herr one's fur international flights. Ya'all will now be hoppin' up tha west coast of tha United States. Yur gonna haff ta go ta tha fur side of this floor, down three flights of escalators, through the revolving glass doors and git on one of those cute, little, red transit buses that'll tack ya ta tha other terminal. Ya'all shud be thur in about 50 minutes." You can just imagine the chaos I created going through that airport. Not to mention the lady I nearly killed when I knocked her off the escalator.

In order to get through the revolving glass doors, I had to make three trips with my luggage. Then I had to dodge traffic to get to the "cute" little, red transit bus. It had automatic folding doors; they closed at least a dozen times on me and my gear.

Eventually, I reached the right terminal and my plane. The airline stewardess there was wonderful; completely organized, crisp, and efficient.

She stowed my luggage, ushered me through to the "first class" section, placed my silly hat in the overhead rack, sat me in a big, comfortable, lazy-boy-type chair, and in a soft, soothing voice said, "We are so sorry for the inconvenience. We have upgraded you to first class. Your entire trip today is at our expense. Sit back, relax, and enjoy the flight. What can I get you to drink dear?"

I nearly hugged her. "I don't usually drink this early in the day." I said. "But today, I will have a double rum and coke." Each time the glass was empty, the wise woman brought me another one. I don't know how many I had. I lost count. But, I do know, that I was extremely relaxed and mellow when I reached the next airport; which was a good thing.

As soon as we landed, Miss Efficiency was back. "Come with me and we'll get you off first." she said. As I went to go through the door, she gently touched my elbow. "Try to relax and stay calm," she said. Warning bells should have gone off in my head. Why was she saying this? However, the rum had made me oblivious to any problems and I simply did not care, at that point, what she meant.

A really old, creepy guy came on board, and gathered my luggage. He threw it, and me, on a golf-cart-like vehicle. In his brown, baggy coveralls, with a massive, straggly mane of dirty brown hair, and a full beard, he reminded me of the lion in the Wizard of Oz.

With the cart overloaded, and tipping precariously, he shot off through a labyrinth of dirty, dark tunnels beneath the airport. He never talked. He never explained where we were going. He just sped along, totally ignoring my questions, until, after what felt like an eternity, we eventually crashed through two saloon-like doors and popped up on the runway.

It had turned into a dark and stormy day. Through the wind and rain, I saw a plane. Oh, a very small plane. The kind, I thought, that rock stars charter, like Buddy Holly. Remembering his untimely death, I was now terrified.

A rather large man, about 300 pounds, shouted in a deep loud gruff voice, "I`m ready to go. So, gid on board Mrs. Suck." I thought it best not to correct him. He threw my luggage into a compartment under the plane and kicked the latch door shut. Laughing, he said, "I hope that holds shut or we'll be spewing yer stuff all over the country." This was not a comforting thought.

As I took the first step, he said, "I'm yer baggage man." I took another step. "And I'm yer flight attendant." I took another step. "And I'm yer pilot, Bob." He laughed uproariously at his own joke. I had absolutely no confidence he could even get the plane off the ground.
I basically crawled on to that plane. Not just because I was drunk, tired and scared, - the door was only three feet high. There were six seats. Two rather shady, gangster-looking

23

men were already in the seats by the far window. They scowled at me, and turned away. Bob ordered me to sit in the seat directly behind him. "It will balance the plane better," he explained. Of course I sat where he said to sit. I wanted this little plane to be balanced. With the wind and rain blowing so hard, I figured we needed every advantage we could get.

There was no overhead rack, so I continued to wear my Chinese hat. It perched on my head like some poor excuse for a hard hat, and certainly would not have protected me if we had fallen from the sky.

Over the roar of the sputtering engines, Bob shouted out, "You better put on your seat belts!" Then he laughed. There were no seat belts. I started to pray. I never stopped praying as the lightning flashed within inches of the plane and the rain continued to fall so hard and heavy that you could not see anything. I watched the one working windshield wiper slowly and ineffectively move across the front window and was positive that Bob could not see either. He started to whistle "We Shall Overcome." This did not help my escalating panic.

Over the next few hours, we somehow shook, shimmied, and shuddered our way across the Canadian border and landed in Vancouver. When I realized the plane had indeed held together and we had landed, I breathed a huge sigh of relief.

Bob lowered the door. Sounding like John Wayne, I heard his gruff voice say, "Watch the lip on that door." I heard it,

just as my foot caught the lip on that door, and I went tumbling down the stairs, and on to the pavement.
"A little anxious to leave are we, Mrs. Suck?" Bob gleefully chuckled.

As I picked myself up, I noticed that I had ripped the knee right out of my left pant leg. The sleeves of my jacket were wet and dirty from resting on the filthy runway. My hat had fallen off and by the time I loaded up my luggage, my hair was soaked from the pouring rain. I looked like a wet cat.
At this point, they literally had me run, from one end of that airport to the other, with airline personnel stationed along the route, shouting out my name. "This way Mrs. Suck." "Mrs. Suck. Mrs. Judy Suck. This way!" About eight of them flagged me through. Finally, breathless, totally dishevelled and extremely exhausted, I reached my plane. Four flight attendants rushed to grab my luggage. As I rushed down the aisle, people stared at me in disbelief, disappointment and disgust. After waiting for 30 minutes, with the engines running, they were expecting the Prime Minister, a movie star, or at least some celebrity. Instead they got a wet, wino-looking woman, who was a wee bit inebriated. And she was coming to first class. I didn't care about their nasty looks. Or mine for that matter. I figured that I was getting close to home.

The meal was delicious, the wine superb and the cheese cake divine. But, nothing was as beautiful as the lights of the city of Mississauga, as we flew into Toronto's Pearson International Airport that night. I had no luggage to claim and no lines to stand in. Two airline officials carried my bags and escorted me through to a door where my husband was waiting. He looked me up and down, and without even cracking a smile, he asked, "So, how was your trip?"

Because, I have a sense of humour, and the ability to laugh at myself, I was able to reply, "I just survived an unbelievable adventure, Mr. Suck."

Isn't laughter wonderful? I hope that you laughed out loud. In the face of adversity, laughter definitely lightened the load for me. From this story, learn not only to laugh at life's little adventures, (some people might call them disasters), but, to also share your story with others. Help them have a good laugh too.

The more embarrassing the story, the better people like it. I was the Director of Human Resources and running a really important meeting. Attendees included Presidents of various companies and Lawyers. I worked for months on getting everything ready. On the day of the meeting, which I was chairing, I put on a new navy blue dress and beautiful red jacket and my navy blue shoes. I really thought I looked great. That night when I got home, I went to put away my shoes. I looked in the closet at my shoe rack. I wondered why there was a space a shoe, then another space. Why not two spaces together, waiting for my shoes. I looked down at my feet. I had on one black shoe and one navy blue shoe. They were not even the same style. One was plain the other scooped. The heels were different heights. No one had said a word!

Judy Suke

The next morning when I went into the office, I scowled at the Receptionist, and said, "I'm mad at you." As I ran into different people throughout the day, I kept saying, "I'm mad at you." At 1:00 p.m. they all came into my office. The spokesman for the group said, "You never get mad at us. What's up?"

I explained what I had done the day before and complained that no one said anything. Of course, no one had noticed. They howled at my mistake, which they thought was particularly funny in front of such prestigious guests. Not only did it lighten the load that day, every time I wore that dress and jacket, people came in and peeked under my desk to see if my shoes matched.

Laughter is the most wonderful, inexpensive gift that you can give. I encourage you to give it often.

"You have the ability to arouse various emotions in me: please select carefully."
-   *Jane Seabrook, Author, 'Furry Logic'*

Chapter 3

Deftly Dealing With Difficult People

Dealing with difficult people, difficult situations and conflict is a subject that is important for each and every one of us, because, it is part of life. These difficult people and these difficult situations help to reveal our strengths and build our character. The quicker we learn the lessons, the sooner we get to move on. If we don't grow in our ability to handle things, we keep experiencing them again and again and again and again.

Throughout my life, whatever I was doing, as a customer service representative, an executive administrator, a technical sales representative, an office manager, a division sales manager, a human resources manager, a trainer, a college professor, (Sounds like I could not keep a job – but, I am just really old and get bored easily and moved on purpose.) a volunteer, a wife and mother... I feel that I've met more than my share of difficult people. What about you?

What I have come to realize is that, no matter what your position in life, or your occupation in the work world, you will have to deal with difficult people, difficult situations and conflict. In this chapter, I am going to give you tips so that you can get control, keep control, and gain cooperation ... in a *nice way.*

First, who are these difficult people? Oh, their physical appearance may vary, but here are some traits that they share:

- They **CRITICIZE**, they **SULK**, they **COMPLAIN**
- They can be **NEGATIVE and STUBBORN**
- **RESISTING, DISAGREEING and OPPOSING** without apparent reason.
- They tend to blow things out of proportion, and then they **overreact**.
- They are people who **look for faults** as if hunting for buried treasure, and then they can **find something wrong with everything** and everyone in their lives
- They feel compelled to point out and **correct the errors of others**.
- When given a leadership role, they insist on trying to get the most out of others by being **ornery, even ruthless.**

By doing all of these things, they create negative feelings and morale problems and they can do a pretty good job of making your life miserable, if you let them. Do you recognize someone like that? Are *you* someone like that?

The secret to peace is controlling how you react to the situations. In life, you will meet many different kinds of people. Some you will click with and some you will clash with. The ones you clash with – will

> **Cold Hard Fact: Stress is not caused by a person or a situation – it is caused by your reaction to the person or situation. Therefore, it is your fault.**

cause you to become each other's difficult person. **Yes, we are all someone's difficult person.**

I am a perky, positive mental attitude kind of person. I drive the pessimists crazy. (They call themselves realists and think I am ridiculously positive.) I make decisions fast, based on gut instinct, and I am usually right - drives the methodical people and analytical-thinkers nuts.

When I was a teenager I worked in a factory. The first day they showed me how the machine worked. That night as I was going to sleep, I thought of a better rhythm for doing my work. The next day I happily increased my production. The day after that I did even more. As I was being paid for piece work, I thought I was pretty smart. A few days later, as I walked back from the lunch room, a rather large woman pinned me up against the wall. She had her arm across my neck. I found it hard to breath. She did not seem to care. She explained that while I only had to keep up my speed during the summer, the regular employees would have to keep up the pace all year. I agreed to slow down.

From that experience I learned three things: facing a problem head on is important, honesty is important, brute force is not necessary. Remember those three things, they drive everything.

Communication – The Key to Handling Difficult People
When we communicate face-to-face, experts have determined that the actual words we use, though very

31

important, represent only a small percentage of our total communication. Here are the figures:

Words We Use	=	*7%*
Tone of Voice	=	*38%*
Body Language	=	*55%*

What these figures tell us is that indirect communication has a greater impact than you might have imagined. When you were a child, I bet your mother had a "look". You would be in public, she would glare at you and although no words were spoken, the message was clear. "You better stop that. I won't hit you here, but wait till we get home." In other words, watch the body language. Even when you are not saying anything – you are sending a powerful message.

Facial Expressions ...
Frowning, basically says "go away", "you're nuts", "I don't like you or what you said or what you're doing". Not a good look to gain cooperation.

Pouting makes you look childish and ridiculous. Some people actually resemble a fish when they pout. It is definitely a bad choice when you want to get control. No one wants to give in to a childish person.

Smiling on the other hand gives you the power to say anything. You can be honest and get away with it. Picture a big smile and someone saying, "That annoyed me. Why'd you do it?"

What happens when you say this is they have one of two responses. Either, they explain why they did it their way, and it no longer annoys you, or they reply, "I had no idea that would annoy you. How do you want it done?" This clears it up and you are no longer bothered by it all.

Body Language ...
Folded arms, clearly say, "I do not want to listen to you or hear your opinion." "I don't care what you have to say." Spreading your arms out with open hands, invites discussion. (Possibly more than you want. But, it is a good idea to let people talk.)

Posture ...
Head down, eyes towards the floor, gives you a mopey, sad appearance. The look says, "I can't handle this. Life is terrible."

Head up, shoulders back, making eye contact, and the world knows you are confident and in control. The look says, "I can handle anything. Life is great!"

Body language can even affect the way you feel ...
Try this: LOOK DOWN - HANDS IN LAP – FROWN Say "I'm happy." STAND UP – ARMS UP - SMILE – Shout, "I'm miserable."
See. You cannot fool the body with the words you use. The gestures have more power.

Eye Contact adds sincerity, and shows you care. When you are talking to someone, don't be looking all over the place to see who else there is to talk to, look at the person you are speaking with.

Tone of Voice *gives your true feelings away.* Often we are unaware of our tone. Ask your spouse or other family members and they will be more than willing to point out your flaws. If you were here in front of me, I could demonstrate this point. Because you are not, you will have to use your imagination to remember a time when someone used a tone that hurt your feelings. Maybe, it was your mother, or a teacher, or a friend. When someone is upset, they have a right to be upset and it does not help if you say, "I did not mean it that way." Obviously, it came across in a hurtful way. Remember, what people think they hear, is what they hear, and what you say is not always what they hear.

Prompt Feedback is *important.* Hesitate and your sincerity is gone. When a woman says, "Do I look fat in these pants?" How quickly her spouse answers could make a difference between a happy household, or a cold shower. When someone asks, "Can you help me with this?" Right away you should say, "Of course. I would love to help you." Then be realistic. "I just have to finish this project and will get back to you at 4:00" (Or Friday or next week – whatever is realistic.)

Other people are affected by your energy – or lack of it. Energy is always there. It is around you. People feel it. Have you met someone for the first time, and even though they have not said a word, you are thinking, "I don't like her." You just know that you don't like them. It is because of their energy field meeting your energy field and bouncing off you. Or you are in the boardroom and someone walks in and you immediately think, "I was

Judy Suke

hoping she wouldn't come." Why? – Because their energy is bad and sucks the energy out of the room. They are what I call "BMW People"; people who are always bitching, moaning and whining. Then someone else enters and you think, "Oh I'm glad she is here. Things always go well when she is here." That is because she has great positive energy. Our energy is created by our thoughts. So, think positive powerful good thoughts.

People are also affected by your words – encouraging or critical; by your actions – friendly, cold, or indifferent; and by your attitude – positive or negative. What you say to the cab driver, the sales clerk, clients, suppliers, fellow employees, or your boss has a ripple effect. Cut somebody off in traffic – they could be in a foul mood all day. Smile at someone on the way to work; it could make their day.

Increase your awareness. How are you affecting the people around you? Take control of your actions. Each morning ask yourself, "What do I want to create and experience today?" "What atmosphere do I need to create?"

If it is a stressful time – year end in accounting – closing time for a bid in engineering - let people know, you know what they are going through, and that you care. (Sometimes you may need to fake it.)

Embroidery on a Pillow:
"If momma ain't happy,
ain't nobody happy."
In life, male or female, you are like the Momma in your world.

35

Don't Sweat the Small Stuff

Best-selling author, Richard Carlson, Ph.D. says, "There are two rules for living in harmony... # 1 Don't sweat the small stuff.   # 2 It's all small stuff."

There are no guarantees when you don't sweat the small stuff. Your life will not be perfect, but you will learn to accept life with far less resistance. Don't waste your energy - choose your battles wisely. Being contented and happy also will upset others who are jealous and that makes it worthwhile.

Be Honest

From the book 'Don't Sweat the Small Stuff'
"Stop sweeping your frustrations under the rug. Let your steam out lightly by speaking what's on your mind, when it's on your mind – in a gentle way."

We actually travel through life with our thoughts as navigator. Scary isn't it. If you let your thoughts get out of control, you start to assume the worst and can overreact. There was a secretary. (I won't give the name) At 11:00 a.m. her boss came to her and said he needed an important report completed for a meeting the next day. She said, "No problem." He left for the day to attend a conference. Right after he left, disaster struck. The receptionist went home sick and the secretary had to cover her role. The copy machine broke down and she was the only one who knew how to fix it. Things were crazy all day and she did not get to the report. She would have stayed late to work on it, but, her husband was out of town and she had to pick the kids up at the daycare. She rushed

Judy Suke

home, made supper, bathed the kids and got them to bed. When her husband arrived home she was banging the dishes around as she washed them, screaming at the cat and was anxious and upset. He was concerned and asked what was going on. She explained about the report and her fear that the boss would be horribly upset. Her husband immediately was on the defensive for her, he said, "Don't you let him yell at you." He hugged her. "You work very hard and often stay late, and do errands for him on your lunch hour. You stand up to him and don't take any crap." (Those were his exact words not mine.) Of course when she went to bed, she could not sleep. She was too worried about the report. She got up early, asked her husband to get the kids to school and daycare, and headed into work. She was working on the report, when her boss came in at 9:00. He smiled. She didn't let that fool her. He said, "Good morning, Judy." (Oh, I was not going to give you her name.) She did not let that fool her. She gave him a harsh look and growled, "I did not get the report done. The receptionist went home sick, the copy machine broke down, clients wanted answers and you were out. I had to handle it all. I just started the report." She straightened her shoulders and gave him a challenging stare. He looked at her calmly and asked, "Can it be done by noon?" "Yes." She replied. "No problem then," he said. "My meeting is at 2:00." This was wasted energy on an imagined catastrophe; and lots of worry over nothing. The trouble is that we feel emotions just as strongly from situations we IMAGINE. Don't allow emotions and worries to sit and simmer and get worse. If you are worried about something ...a meeting of the bosses behind a closed door ...

someone's reaction to something you did ... the reason someone else did something ... just ask them about it, be honest, and face it head on.

Whatever you do, don't speak to everyone else except the difficult person. Nothing is worse than hearing someone repeat, word for word, what you should not have said in the first place.

**If you wouldn't write it, and sign it,
and hang it on the wall by your desk, don't say it.**

Seek First to Understand; Then Be Understood.
Many years ago at a leadership training camp (I was in high school at the time) I heard a story about a difficult person. It went something like this ... A business woman got into a cab one day at rush hour. She was hurrying to catch a train and she suggested a route to the station. "Yo Lady, I've been a cab driver for 20 years. You think I don't know the best way to go!" the driver yelled. She tried to explain that she had not meant to offend him, but the more she tried the louder the driver yelled. She finally realized that he was too upset to be reasonable. So, she did the unexpected. "You are absolutely right." She told him. "It must seem dumb for me to assume that you don't know the best way through the city." Shocked by the change in tone, the driver quit yelling, gave his passenger a confused look in the rear-view mirror, turned down the very road she had suggested and got her to the train on time.

Throughout our lives, we all have to deal with people like the cab driver, who overreact, and blow things out of proportion. There is this irresistible urge to dig in our heels and say, "That is not what I meant. You totally misunderstood me. You have no reason to be upset." Now, isn't that what an upset person wants to hear? Instead, like the business woman, we should find something to agree with, to quiet them down and gain control of the situation. From my own experience, I can tell you that sometimes you have to listen really, really closely to find that truth. It is definitely worth the effort though – because once you give up your need to control the situation, your need to be the only one who is right ... and find something to agree with – they will become less defensive, relax and listen to you. Stephen Covey in his book, *"The Seven Habits of Highly Effective People"*, describes empathetic listening as *LISTENING TO UNDERSTAND.* (Most people listen to speak.)

HOW TO LISTEN to UNDERSTAND:
Stop talking: Sounds obvious; unfortunately, emotional people tend to talk at the same time.

Stop thinking about what you are going to say next: How can you possibly hear what they are saying if you are busy thinking.

Do not interrupt: That is just plain rude and annoying. Let them explain their whole point of view. The part you might be able to agree with could be at the very end.

Do not finish their sentences: I am guilty of this. I am a fast talker. I like to move the conversation along at a fast pace. When I am talking to someone who is talking slowly, I just want to crank them up and get things moving. So, I jump in and finish their sentences. Sometimes it works and they say, "Yes that is what I meant." Mostly, it annoys them. "No that's not what I meant." Not only does my interruption and finishing their sentences frustrate them and cause the situation to worsen, but, it also steals my energy. Do you have any idea how hard it is to carry both sides of the conversation? Besides, if you are speaking for the other person – how can you be sure that you really turned them to your way of thinking?

ONE OF LIFE'S LITTLE RULES: **Conflicts are going to happen. They are part of the process.**

However, you can learn to recognize, understand and take appropriate action to use the conflict to your advantage. Conflict can be good. It can broaden the discussion; help to reach a wider understanding of what's needed; and even lead to improved procedures.

REMEMBER THE SERENITY PRAYER:
"God grant me the SERENITY to accept the things I cannot change; the COURAGE to change the things I can; and the WISDOM to know the difference."
- *Reinhold Neibuhr*

(I add - And give me the authority to get my way.)

Judy Suke

Chapter 4
Aging Isn't for Sissies

That wonderful actress, the late Betty Davis, said "Aging Isn't for sissies." As I grow older I realize that she was absolutely right. Aging gives us some tough challenges. Trust me a sense of humour will help you there.

From personal experience I know **the mind slows** and sometimes goes to Florida without me. Not good when you are a speaker. I look at the audience and say, "What was I talking about?" Even normal words are not there.

One day I was teaching a lesson and I wanted to use an example. My mind was totally blank. I looked at the audience and pleaded, "Help me." I described a man in uniform; "flat hat - red jacket - baggy pants and high black boots." They shouted back ... "Mountie!" They were right. Another trainer commended me on being so playful with the audience. I said, "OK" (Let's say that it was planned.)

Which reminds me of a great joke:
Two older-aged couples get together for dinner and cards. The wives prepared the meal and as per custom the guys are washing up the dishes. Mike says, "We went out to a great restaurant the other night. The food was good and the prices were reasonable, the place was fixed up nice with candle-light and it impressed the wife."
Bob asks, "What was the name of the restaurant?"

41

Mike sounds disgusted with himself and says, "I can't remember." After a minute he asks, "What is the name of that pretty flower with the thorns?" Bob says, "You mean a Rose?" Mike walks over to the living-room door and shouts, "Rose, what was the name of the restaurant we went to Monday night?"

When the mind goes blank it is not good for cooking either. I used to stand there looking at the recipe asking myself, "Did I already put the cup of sugar in?" Now, I line up the ingredients, and put them away as I use them. This saves a lot of disasters, but not all, I'm just not a great cook.

As we age **the hearing goes** or people are whispering to annoy me. I have to shout at some of my friends because they are too proud to wear hearing aids. And then there is Ethel. She farts at inappropriate times because she can't hear it and she thinks no one else can. I never want to be the volunteer chosen to take her to church.

Another issue with aging is **the vision dims** – and blurs – and bifocals make me dizzy. When I first got my bifocals, I came out of the optometrist's office and walked right into a sign post, and then I tripped off the curb. I could not even focus people's faces, so I decided to say an enthusiastic "Hi" to total strangers, just in case I knew them. I already looked drunk; I didn't want to look rude too!

I have noticed that many people, not just me, have **bones that creak, ache, and break easily**. And then they

Judy Suke

don't heal very fast. I have issues and aches that have gone on for years. I sit down to breakfast and hear "snap, crackle, and pop" and I don't eat Rice Krispies.

Some days **it is hard just moving.** I suffer from arthritis. When I wake up, my body won't move. My knees refuse to support me, and walking straight is impossible. If I wake up in the middle of the night, I stagger toward the bathroom. One night, I bounced off the dresser, managed to push my way past a chair and then accidentally lost my balance and ended up in the closet. From across the room I heard my husband say, "You do know that you are in the closet, right?" And I thought he slept through everything.

They say with age comes wisdom. That doesn't make up for the beer bellies, the sagging boobs and the cellulite.

There are so many **things that SAG.** The skin on my face is sliding off and dropping below my chin creating more chins. My breasts are heading toward my waist. I have learned that, not only do they sag; they slide under the arm pits. This totally ruined my golf game. I bought an expensive bra, a feat of engineering, made by NASA. It has great strength and lifts and pushes them in and up and out of the way. It is worth every penny.

The arms sag and flap in the wind. I read somewhere ... "in mid-life – women no longer have upper arms – they have wing spans." We are like flying squirrels in drag. Picture that.

Of course there is the **weight gain**. I see my reflection in the window and think ... Who is that big bold broad? There is a skinny girl inside of me, crying to get out; I can usually shut her up with a piece of cheesecake. I have discovered, to get rid of the **wrinkles** – just eat until they fill out. (Ya – skinny people show more wrinkles.) They look older, sooner. So there! There is an advantage to being full-figured. I like that phrase, **full-figured.** It's like skinny people are only half there. Not finished yet. The advantage is, my grandchildren like to cuddle into my nice big bosom. One day my granddaughter heard me complaining about trying to lose weight. She ran over, climbed into my lap, hugged me and said, "You are just what a grandma should be." Why would I want to change?

In Mid-life we ask ourselves those tough questions ...
What is the meaning of life?
Why am I here?
How much healthy choice ice cream can I eat before it's no longer a healthy choice?

As I have aged, I've noticed that **it takes so much longer to put my make-up on.** The sales people have convinced me to use products to cleanse, refresh, and moisturize ...using loving gestures to get into all the craggily old corners of my face. Then there is the eye lifter cream "stuff", and then concealer ... I used to use a little concealer on blemishes, now I spread it all over my face to cover the age spots (which I cannot see without my glasses). Then there is the foundation, and translucent powder, and blush etc etc etc. I stop and wonder ... did I

Judy Suke

put the moisturizer on? Do I need to start over? I am going to have to line it up in order and put it away as I use it.

I recently had all of my upper teeth removed and **dentures** put in, on the same day. He had a little trouble and it felt like he was digging in my sinuses. There were a lot of stitches and it was very painful. But, he gave me Percocet – then I didn't care about the pain or anything else for that matter. I had trouble adjusting to the dentures and speaking was strange. My husband and daughter were not sympathetic. They kept asking me to say things with s's in them and then they would laugh hysterically. "Mississauga", "Mississippi", "seals swimming smoothly". Then my husband, using the voice of Sylvester the cat, said, "Say suffering succotash." Remember the law says that I can't kill him, and I was in terrible pain, so I said, (Excuse the language) "Go to hell." Remember – terrible pain. That sobered him up. He said, "Well you can say that plainly."

I have a friend who is 90. One day she said to me, "If you are smiling, you can tell someone to go to hell." Of course I said, "Doris, who are you telling to go to hell?" She said, "The ladies at the church." I said, "Aren't you afraid that they will get mad at you?" She said, "There is no peer pressure at 90." So, when you want to be brutally honest with people, smile. Then you can say anything.

I spend a lot of time thinking about the hereafter. I go all the way upstairs - then wonder, "What am I here after?" I figure if I walk downstairs, I will remember. Then, I get to

45

the bottom of the stairs and wonder, "What am I here after?" There is a story going around on the internet and it totally reminds me of my own example: I can't seem to stay focused. My **mind wanders.** Typical day: I decide to go to the store for some bread. It takes me ten minutes to find the keys. It must be the husband. He doesn't put them where they belong. On the way to the garage, I notice my plants are dying and desperately need water. I set down my purse and head to my office to get the watering can, (don't ask). I figure while I'm there I should check the emails. But, I can't find my glasses. I see a coffee cup from yesterday that I forgot to take to the kitchen. I grab it and head to the kitchen. As I head to the kitchen, I decide if I'm heading downstairs, I should take the hamper down and put in a load of laundry. When I get to the laundry room, I notice the TV remote is there. (Oh ya; I hid it to tease my husband.) I throw in a load of laundry and try to remember what I needed to do next. I take the remote towards the family room, and hear the phone ringing. I go to the kitchen and grab the phone. It is my friend wondering why I don't answer my emails. We talk for a few minutes; then the phone goes dead. I remember I was supposed to get a new battery last week. Then I head down the hall, trying to remember what it was I was planning to do. At the end of the day, we have no bread; I can't find my purse; there is a wet load of laundry sitting in the washer; I still can't find my glasses, the plants look dead; and I don't remember what I did with the car keys. When I try to figure out why nothing got done, I'm really baffled, because I know I was busy all day long, and I'm really tired. That's my life.

Judy Suke

When we are old, **we value our really good friends.** We are dedicated to each other. We understand each other and empathize with each other. They say ... "A good friend will help you move. A great friend will help you move a body." That's just my menopause talking. Seriously though, sometimes don't you just want to kill someone? There are people in my life today, simply because it is illegal to kill them.

Aging is frustrating; you finally get your life together, your head on straight, figure everything out, things are going smoothly, and along comes **menopause.** You can't get through a day without meeting someone who is ... stupid. You're waiting in a line-up, watching someone ineptly try to do something. You can't help but be annoyed. You are not saying it out loud, (you are Canadian), but you are thinking, "She could have done that differently. She could have done that better. I could do it so much better." Basically, we just want people to do things the right way; our way. Once you accept that there is more than one right way to do most things, you will have less stress in your life. I suggest that you look at the outcome instead of the process. When you feel like you want to kill them ... walk away. Killing is illegal.

Sign of Menopause # 1
You sell your home heating system at a yard sale
> Someone told me, it's not hot flashes; it's your inner child playing with matches. I like that image.   —
> Sounds mischievous

Sign of Menopause # 2
You change your underwear after a sneeze. And get out of bed three times a night.

Sign of Menopause # 3
You have to write post-it notes with your kid's names on them. You need name tags at family gatherings.

Sign of Menopause # 4
You need to write everything down or it doesn't get done. You have lists – then forget to look at the lists

Sign of Menopause # 5
You wish that life was like a computer, and you could press Ctrl Alt Delete - and start things over.

Sign of Menopause # 6
You cry easily and at inappropriate times. Then you are mad because you cried.

Sign of Menopause # 7
You have turned into the (excuse the language) bitch from hell. And you make no apologies.

Sign of Menopause # 8
You notice that your children have turned into you ... and you don't like them.   But your grandchildren are perfect.

We are going to age; we have no choice. I think we can do it and have fun along the way. Here are some tips:

Laugh at Jokes:
Example: Oh To Be 12 Again....

A man was sitting on the edge of the bed, observing his wife, looking at herself in the mirror. Since her birthday was not far off, he asked what she'd like to have for her birthday. "I'd like to be twelve again", she replied, still looking in the mirror. On the morning of her birthday, he arose early, made her a nice big bowl of Coco Pops, and then took her to the theme park. What a day! He put her on every ride in the park; the Death Slide, the Corkscrew, the Wall of Fear, the Screaming Monster Roller Coaster, everything there was. Five hours later they staggered out of the theme park. Her head was reeling and her stomach felt upside down. He then took her to a McDonald's where he ordered her a Happy Meal with extra fries and a chocolate shake. Then it was off to the cinema with popcorn, a huge Cola, and her favourite sweets......M&M's. What a fabulous adventure! Finally she wobbled home with her husband and collapsed into bed exhausted. He leaned over his wife with a big smile and lovingly asked, 'Well dear, what was it like being twelve again?' Her eyes slowly opened and her expression suddenly changed. "I meant my dress size, you jerk!!!!" The moral of the story: Even when a man is listening, he is gonna get it wrong.

Live in the Present

Forgive people. It takes way too much of your energy to stay angry. It depletes your strength and takes away your health. Simply tell them that you forgive them for that horrible thing that they did. (That way they feel bad and you feel good.)

The past is dead and gone. Whatever happened, happened, it cannot be undone. So move on. Let it go. Think of what you want now.

I was speaking at a retreat and I overheard a women say that she hadn't talked to her mother or sister in years. Family means everything to me; I could not imagine doing that. I asked her, "What happened that was bad enough to cause you to do this?" She replied, "I don't remember, but, I'm not calling them until they call me." I looked at her shocked and said, "The curiosity would kill me. At least call them and find out if anyone remembers what happened. If it is bad enough you can get mad again. If no one remembers, get over it and get on with life."

What a waste of energy. I don't waste my time on anger, resentment, jealousy, or any of the other negative emotions. I don't have that much energy to spare.

Be Likable

Smile at the world. Show you care. At the end of the day, if you feel that the world is full of miserable people, look in the mirror. What you are sending out, is what you are drawing in. Smiling is easier than frowning and it is infectious.

Picture this:

The optimist jumps out of her bed in the morning, runs to the window, raises her face to the warmth of the sun and says, "Good morning, God." The pessimist drags his butt out of bed, shuffles over to the window; squints his eyes against the brightness of the same sun, and says, "Good God, morning." Who do you think is going to have the better day?

At least start your day in a positive way. If you wake up in pain, pretend you are a cat and stretch. Anytime you are in pain or sad, don't concentrate on it; don't talk constantly about it, find something to do to take your mind off of it. Focus on something else, funny movies, music, a good book. Make a list of all the things you are grateful for. Say affirmations, "It is going to be a great day."

Lighten Up - Have Fun
Old people have a reputation for being CRANKY, GRUMPY and DIFFICULT. We see the stress on their faces; the eyebrows are at an angle, the eyes are squinting, they are frowning. Basically, they look constipated. Then they grunt, and groan and ... sigh heavily. Who wants to be around that? I challenge you to smile and have fun instead. Share your funny stories. Laugh at them yourself, every time you tell them.

In her book "*Life is Not a Stress Rehearsal*" Loretta La Roche says, "Your inner child is probably miserable because your outer adult isn't having any fun." You need to have fun. Wear fun ties, funky jewellery, bright colours and silk or satin underwear. The Red Hat Society ladies have it perfectly right.

If you have forgotten how to have fun, follow around the children. Do what they do. I was babysitting my grandson. I

51

had just finished bathing him, and the little devil got away before I could dry him off. There he was, naked and wet, leaping and laughing, and squealing with delight and running through the house. I thought, "That looks like fun." So, I tried it. My husband caught me. He said, "What will the neighbours think?" I said, "I don't know I haven't shown them yet." Check it out.

Sometimes the internet brings us some wise sayings. I love this one:

Life should not be a journey to the grave with the intention of arriving safely in an attractive and well-preserved body ... but rather to skid in sideways, chocolate in one hand, wine in the other, body thoroughly used up, totally worn out and screaming, "Woo Hoo what a ride!"

Judy Suke

PART II

By Meg Soper

About the Author:

Meg is an expert on the subject of striking balance within our hectic lives.

Over the past three decades she has worked as a Registered Nurse; become one of Canada's foremost stand-up comediennes, and raised a family.

Meg has taken the life lessons learned while travelling this unique path to become a much sought after professional speaker and trainer. She blends her unique insights with unforgettable humour to help people develop practical strategies for work and life.

Meg has appeared as a keynote speaker and feature performer at conventions and corporate functions across North America and internationally. She has shared the stage with such celebrities as Ray Romano, and Ellen Degeneres. She has appeared on the CBC Television Network, Women's Television Network, and Prime TV, as well as being featured in many radio programs and comedy festivals.

Meg Soper Presentations
www.megsoper.com
905-825-9339

INTRODUCTION

The road leading all of us comes with its share of twists and turns. The challenge is to seek out love and support along the way to stay the course, or change direction – and somehow end up in one piece in a good place. Suffice it to say that I ended up where I am because of the values instilled in me by my parents, who demonstrated a spirit that said never give up.

After 27 years in the healthcare industry as a Registered Nurse and many years on the road as a stand-up comic I now enjoy a successful career as a professional humorous speaker and trainer. Being married, raising a family and living with two teenagers has also inspired the maintenance of a healthy sense of humour.

In the next few chapters I am going to share some of my life story, observations and a few of the lessons learned on a rather convoluted journey as I hit another milestone in life: The Big Five Oh! Somehow I thought I had all the answers when I was 20, but the fact is that the most important things I have learned in my life have been through others. The friends, family, colleagues, patients, clients, audience members and people I have met by chance have all made a difference in my life in some way.

It is no surprise then that our personalities are a complicated mosaic that are always in flux, and dictate how we respond to life's everyday happenings.

The succession of curve balls through life keeps coming. We know there will be plenty of "hits and misses" – but as long as you are learning along the way, making the necessary adjustments, and keeping your sense of humour then you will find that you can deal effectively with anything that happens to come your way.

Perhaps the biggest lesson of all was served up right in front of me as I watched my parents deal with the tragic loss of my brother, and just a number of years later lose their business and our family home. They had each other, and somehow they managed to bounce back. They adapted their life style and their perspective ... they simply never gave up.

Nobody said it would be an easy ride...they just promised it would be worth it!

Meg Soper

Chapter 5

Laughter is an Anaesthetic

That I have a career in healthcare was the result of an unfortunate and unexpected event. The year was 1982 and I was between 2nd and 3rd year at Queens University in Kingston, Ontario, where I was studying Physical Health Education.

To that point in my life, I had not voluntarily set foot in a hospital. I was travelling in Europe with a close friend when my parents called with some shocking news. The economic downturn in BC resulted in my father losing his business, and as a result they were not going to be able to afford to continue to send me to University in Ontario.

As they say, necessity is the mother of invention. I knew I needed to change lanes, and in particular, I needed to choose a career that would enable me to become financially self-sufficient within a reasonably short timeframe. That phone call changed everything. While I was worried about my parents, it suddenly opened up a new world of possibility. The disappointment of having to leave my life at Queens was a blow, but now I had been given a challenge that I needed to rise up to. During the remaining course of my travels, I met a number of nurses. They struck me as independent, confident and financially secure, doing something that made a difference. My new path in life suddenly appeared clear.

I studied Nursing at a Community College in Vancouver and soon the highs and lows of working in healthcare were revealed. In those early days of nursing, I came to realize that we can never take our health for granted. Seeing

57

families coping with a sick loved one, day in and day out, was an enormous eye opener. Nursing school also taught me the importance of keeping your sense of humour. It was necessary, not just to help me cope, but it proved immensely beneficial to the patients that I worked with. It was amazing to see how a bit of humour could bring a smile to peoples' faces even when they were frightened or facing a tough battle.

Nursing school proved to be a true challenge. It was nerve wracking dealing with masses of course content while also embarking on our practicum in the real world of the hospital with actual live patients. My first day on duty as a student nurse was to be on the Extended Care Floor, starting promptly at 7:00 a.m. The importance of punctuality had always been emphasized in our family. As you can imagine, leading up to my first day, I was on a mission to ensure I would, indeed, be on time for that first shift.

At the time, I was sharing a three-bedroom house with two roommates and my golden retriever. The evening before, I had taken the step of preparing my first new pristine white nurses uniform by sewing my student nursing badge on securely, and placing it in a plastic bag to carry it to work the next morning. After a fitful sleep, I was up early and greeted by a blast of winter that had coated the outdoors with a thick layer of frost, including the cars parked on the street. When I attempted to unlock my car door, nothing happened. The lock was frozen solid! For several minutes, I tried to make it work, but the key wouldn't budge. Of all the mornings for this to happen…this wasn't a good one. I was now in low level panic with the prospect of being late for my first day of work. So, I ran back into the house, filled the kettle, and ignoring my mother's sage advice, watched for what seemed an eternity as the water came to a boil. I flew out the door with the kettle in hand and proceeded to pour steaming water all over the drivers' door. Surely, now it will open? But No! Even with the aid of hot water the lock wasn't budging. While not prone to the use of foul language, I will admit that a few nasty epithets may have squeaked out during this interlude. It was at this point that an anxious neighbour, one who I had shared approximately one sentence with since moving in the previous year, appeared at their doorway and inquired as to what I was doing. In no mood I bellowed back, as if it weren't obvious enough, "My car door is frozen and I'm trying to thaw it out!" She looked perplexed, but oddly calm before replying, "Ummm, actually, that is my car." I quickly looked to my left and realized that, sure enough, she and I owned the same model vehicle. I took a deep breath, and in an attempt to be as matter of fact as possible, I responded "RIGHT...sorry about that!"

Sheepishly, I slinked over to my car, unlocked the door, used a laminated library card to scrape a six inch circumference of frost from the windshield and proceeded to drive through the city with my face pressed up against the glass in an effort to navigate my way to work. That I made it to the hospital without hitting a pedestrian or running up on the sidewalk is quite remarkable. On arrival, and now officially late, feeling a somewhat escalated level of panic, I dashed to the change room and quickly donned my nursing uniform. It was then that I realized the bag I had brought the uniform in had previously carried several baskets of fresh strawberries. The residual berry juice had, over the course of the night and morning, nicely soaked in to the starch white dress. Just when it seemed things could not get any worse, I realized I had neglected to hem the dress and as such found a network of six inch threads dangling down from the bottom of the uniform. Wow... looking good! Then to top things off, like the proverbial cherry on the ice cream sundae, I realized that I had sewn the "VCC Student Nurse" badge to the back of the outfit. What a sight. There I stood, about to embark on my career as a healthcare professional in charge of real lives, with a strawberry stained white dress, six inch threads trailing down and my student nursing badge attached to my right scapula. It was a blow to my morale, and a rather shaky start to my career, but it does provide good entertainment value. And it goes to prove that ... if you can laugh at it ... you can survive it.

Over the course of the next 27 years there were many days that did not unfold according to plan, but they are outweighed by the numerous patients and colleagues that have made my experience in healthcare incredibly worthwhile. Having spent most of my healthcare career as an Operating Room Nurse, I can say with some authority that the OR, in particular, is a unique environment. It can be rife with pressure, while at the same time, thoroughly rewarding as you know you are making a difference in patients' lives every day.

Humour at Work:
Patients and People Who Made a Memorable Impact

TED

He was the gentleman I was checking in for surgery, who looked over his surgical consent form and declared, "I agree to this procedure as long as it does not interfere with the normal functioning of my penis". He was 84 years old. He was having cataract surgery. I am not making this up. I don't think you COULD make this up. We assured him he was safe and indeed, he was. Ted was still living life to the fullest, and making sure we knew.

JIM

Jim lived with the pain of Rheumatoid Arthritis. But, you wouldn't have known it. His mantra to start each day was 'keep moving and don't complain.' Jim's take on his situation was upbeat, and he felt there was nothing more boring than someone who complains about their health problems. His advice: Know that there is always someone out there with bigger problems than you.

LOU

Lou is the face that people inevitably see when they come to the hospital. He has been employed with the housekeeping department since they poured the concrete foundation... 45 years ago! He is one rough looking character. He's hunched over and has a number of missing teeth. Some days it looks like he might have died, but just forgot to lie down. Yet, he always has a smile on his face, and he greets people the same way whether it's the neurosurgeon or the fellow from maintenance. One day, head down and consumed with thought as I made my way to the hospital, Lou sees me. "Hey" he yells out, and I look up to see him, with an even bigger smile than usual beaming across his face. "You know, I cannot wait until tomorrow!" he says to me. So, naturally I ask, 'Why is that Lou?' He chirps back not missing a beat, "Because I just get better looking every day." If we could only bottle that energy and sell it... it's priceless.

CLARA.

Dear old Clara. She made a lasting impression on me. She was admitted to the Operating Room for an elective procedure, insertion of a pacemaker, under local anaesthetic. Checking her chart, I was astonished to learn she was 101 years old! She had her wits about her, a smile on her face and this glint in her eye. Halfway through the procedure the anaesthetist asked her, "How are you doing Clara... is everything okay?" "Well, you're hurting me a little, but nobody likes a complainer, so I'm alright."

After the procedure, I had the honour of taking her back to her hospital room. I just had to know more about her, so I asked her a few questions as we wheeled her bed down the hallway. She'd been married to the same man for over 65 years. "He passed away a few years ago now, but he's always right here" she said, as she placed her hand over her heart. She had three children and a number grandchildren... all of whom she was smitten with. She had her own career and worked until she was 70 years old. She then told me that the day following the procedure she was to move into a Long Term Care facility. It was her decision. She just didn't want to look after the lawn anymore. By this time, we had made it to her room and I couldn't help but ask her, "What is the secret to your spirit?" To which she replied, "Don't take yourself too seriously... no matter how old you are. Nobody's getting out of this life alive." How is that for perspective?

HEIDI

I met Heidi during her battle with breast cancer. She was admitted for surgery after her diagnosis and I was in the process of checking her in. At that time, I recognized her from her previous operation and we chatted and managed to share a laugh about my escapades that day. I told her how I'd lost my dog on a morning run, and the mayhem that I encountered in recovering the lost creature, and then reporting in late for work. She loved the story. She missed the laughter. She was tired of people asking her about her condition, and how she felt. Her goal was to make the best of each day, no matter how she felt, and on a lot of days she did not feel well at all. Above all she didn't want to be treated any differently because of her illness. She didn't want to become the illness.

I was checking her in for her mastectomy that morning, and I had the good fortune of having a few extra minutes before the operation started. So she invited me to sit with her which was an opportunity that I rarely have in the busy environment of the hospital. What a privilege. We talked about the wig collection she had assembled since undergoing chemo. Her husband loved them. He didn't care if she had hair on her head or not. He loved her just the same. But, he did feel as though he was dating a different character depending on which wig she wore each night. There was the red head "Simone", and there was "Roxy" the blonde and "Juanita" the brunette.

> **It is up to us to choose what we focus on.**
>
> **What do you choose to focus on when life dares you to complain?**

She looked to find fun and humour in the midst of a very difficult situation. Talk about shifting your perspective. She chose to embrace the positive as her way to fight back. As she so bravely put it, "I choose to fight back because you can't get cancer of the spirit."

Clara and Heidi are never far from my thoughts, especially when life dares me to complain. It is people like them – who are facing up to tough challenges – who remind us to keep things in perspective when we face our own difficulties. We know there will be days when the sun will not shine, traffic will be bad, the car will blow a gasket and property taxes will go up, yet again. I like to refer to these untoward events as Opposite Moments – moments in the day that are the opposite of what you would prefer to be experiencing. Opposite Moments are inevitable... and they definitely challenge us.

We all have those days when you know it will be a tough row – where it's hard to throw the covers off. We can shift our perspective when those Opposite Moments arise and life dares us to complain. Put your chest out, lift your chin up, smile and say 'bring it on!'

My career in healthcare has taught me that we can never take our life or our health for granted.

My Career in Nursing:
Lessons Learned Along the Way

- ✓ Always remove the foil wrapper from the suppository before administering it to the patient.
- ✓ Ensure the bedpan is secured directly beneath the commode chair before positioning the patient.
- ✓ Do not place a patient's water glass beside their bedside phone...they will answer their water if they are suddenly awakened by the telephone.
- ✓ When caring for a post-operative bilateral nasal surgery patient...who speaks only Italian...do not attempt to take their temperature orally ... they get upset when you minimize their airway.
- ✓ Avoid asking pre-operative patients if they have any 'last words', before they are put under anaesthesia. This tends to make them feel uneasy.

Chapter 6

The Weight of the World and How to Deal with It

"I have been dieting continuously for over 20 years. By all accounts I should be hanging from a charm bracelet by now." Erma Bombeck

It is up to us to figure out what makes us happy. Recognizing the fact that there will be things we can change, and many things that we cannot, helps us learn to find balance in our lives and live within ourselves. This process of discovery will help us develop life strategies about what we need to do so we can get through the day both personally and professionally.

I ate because I was unhappy. When I was 7 years old my 18 year old brother was killed in a car accident. Our family struggled with the loss for many years. I turned to food for comfort and I could not stop eating ... the pounds piled on. In a few short years, there wasn't anything in the mainstream store I could fit into, and consequently I did my clothes shopping at Shirley K maternity store.

As a young teenager, I was unhappy with my weight so I took some steps to change things. Many of these steps were met with road blocks. I paid hundreds of dollars to go to a weight loss clinic, and sign up for the militaristic reduced calorie regime. Every week you weighed in, had your blood pressure checked, and met with the nurse to discuss any issues you were having with the program, like for example, hunger. If, by chance, you strayed from the

65

designated calorie limit, then you had to write out "I like myself" 100 times. If anything was going to cause me to overeat, that was it. Next!

So, then I saw a magazine advertisement for the "Amazing Weight Loss Answer." Sign me up. I sent in my money and two weeks later, I received a book and a skipping rope in the mail. The book extolled the virtues of an all protein diet, combined with 15 minutes of daily aerobic exercise. Apparently if you followed this program, you would look like the muscle bound couple on the cover of the book in only a few short months. I thought 'this is it,' but after two weeks of eating only steak and eggs, while skipping rope in the garage... I couldn't take it anymore.

At the age of twelve I was one of three students recommended by our school health nurse to attend a summer camp for kids with weight issues. We learned about the Canada Food Guide, serving sizes, weighing food portions. We made fridge magnets saying *"Go Do Something Else"* and *"Stop! Calories Ahead"*. It all started to make sense. There were no silver bullets or shortcuts. Some of the principles I learned at that summer camp are still in my mind today. Over the course of a few months, I focused on the goal of shedding those 25 pounds. On one occasion, I accompanied a fellow camper named Catherine home for lunch. Catherine's goal was to lose 70 pounds that summer. It was a sunny day when we arrived at her home, her mother who was morbidly obese was watching television in their darkened basement with a box of chocolates at her side. It was a scene that was etched forever in my mind. Catherine's food choices consisted of Kool-Aid, white bread and Jell-O. She would have considerable difficulty attaining her goal, because her environment was not conducive to success. Until that point,

I had taken for granted the fact that nutritious food had always been made available to me at home. I realized it was up to me to make a healthy choice. That summer I managed to reach my weight loss goal. This was not the case for Catherine.

To this day, I keep a journal in the kitchen and write down my feelings when I get off track with maintaining a healthy weight. I don't need to write in it every day, but I refer to it often. When I feel engaged and focused in life... I am more inclined to make healthy choices with food. When I feel bored, stressed or unhappy, then I tend to make poor food choices, my weight goes up and I don't feel comfortable in my clothes. Self-awareness has turned out to be one of the most important tools for living a healthy life.

To me, weight management comes down to some essential questions ... How do you feel in your clothes? Are your clothes fitting the way you want? Are your energy levels good? If you can answer these questions in the positive, then you are on the right track. On the other hand, if when you take your clothes off to find 'Fruit of the Loom' tattooed on your belly, you may have some work to do.

Things Learned on the Journey with Maintaining a Healthy Weight

1. **Write it down.** Keeping a journal in the kitchen has made me more aware of my eating habits and the feelings attached to the eating experience.

2. **Chocolate is a good thing.** "For me, life without chocolate is NOT an option!" A little every day in some

form is a bonus. Also, ice cream served in an egg cup gives you the taste, but just enough.

3. **Drink 6-8 glasses of water a day.** Take it in the car when you're driving, and have it at your desk when you are at the computer. We can survive much longer without food than we can without water.

4. *Lose the scale.* The weight scale can sabotage your psyche, and weaken your self-image. A bit dramatic, perhaps? Well, maybe, but I don't think you need a number to tell you how you should feel about your progress. Let your clothes be the judge.

5. **Diets don't work.** As soon as you tell yourself, "I'm going on a diet" then all you can think about is food. I put my faith into Weight Watchers. It's not about what you CAN'T have... it's about what you CAN have. Reasonable serving sizes are the key.

6. **Eat Breakfast.** Even if you don't feel hungry... you need to start your day with something in your stomach. Have a healthy snack (fruit with protein) to get you through to lunch if you are on the run.

7. **Make time for your 30 minutes.** Move around for 30 minutes, 3 – 5 times a week at least... it helps reduce our stress and gets the heart rate up. One of the best investments we ever made as a family was our golden retriever. He demands we take those 30 minutes despite the weather pattern outside.

8. **Avoid eating a big meal 2-3 hours before bedtime.** This gives your body more time to digest the food and paves the way for a more restful sleep.

9. **Wait 15 minutes before having a second helping.** It takes your stomach that long to catch up to your brain. Allow the food to reach your stomach before deciding whether or not you need more.

10. **Let the guilt go.** There is no reason to feel guilty about putting nutritious food into your body. Think of your body, its' value to you, and its' needs whenever you eat. It helps you make healthy choices.

Your 30 Minutes

One of the most important things we can do for ourselves is to set aside time each day to do what is meaningful and enjoyable. I make it my goal to set aside not less than 30 minutes to do what I enjoy. It is my way to lose stress and recharge the batteries.

How do you spend YOUR 30 Minutes? It means different things to different people. It could be walking the dog, working in the garden, riding your bike, reading, singing, dancing, laughing, doing yoga, or writing in a journal.

The key is to make this commitment to you. Set that time aside and treat it as though it were any other appointment. It is one of the best investments you'll make. If you're travelling, pack your journal, your runners, your harmonica, your swimsuit or whatever you need for YOUR 30 Minutes. It has been determined that 60-90% of all illness is stress related. Stress will manifest itself at the cellular level. It shows up in many forms ... from emotional to physical disorders. Whether it is an unhealthy relationship, financial issues or a stressful job, the stress will show up.

A little stress can sometimes be a good thing. It can take us out of our comfort zone and push us beyond our self-imposed limits. But, if the stress continues over a long period of time, and if it is not managed carefully it will manifest itself at the cellular level. I have seen it firsthand in the hospital setting. From heart disease to bowel disorders, it will creep up without warning, and potentially become a serious issue.

Stress is an integral part of our lives to such an extent that we may not recognize it. Think of how cell phones, smart phones and 24/7 connectivity have become such a large part of our lives in the last 5 years? There was a story about a gentleman who had checked himself in to a Relaxation Centre. He had been in the meditation room for a long time, so the staff asked if he was ready to come out. He replied "no I'll be finished my phone call in a few minutes." Until that occurrence it had not been necessary to ban cell phones in the meditation room. For some of us, it is physically difficult to shut down. To turn off the communication and just be in the moment is a challenge.

On a related note, do you find it harder to get a good night sleep after watching TV or working on your computer late into the evening? Well, I do and it turns out that light has a powerful impact on our sleep cycle. When we stare at the bright light of a computer screen our brain takes it as a cue telling us it is time to get up, not shut down and go to bed. Save the email replies for the morning, and read a book or do Yoga for Your 30 Minutes before bed.

Stress Relief Strategies to Consider (or not)

Why I Don't Recommend Golf for Stress Relief
For 30 years I have been a recovering golfer. While I don't recommend golf for stress relief, I do believe it to be a great barometer of an individual's character, particularly

when you witness how they behave during an exceptionally poor round of golf. Steve Smith, better known as Red Green, really said it very well when he stood on the 18th tee at the end of a very bad golf game and announced, "you know I can play a lot better than this... it's just I never have."

Dealing with Teens

One of my co-workers at the hospital swore by one method for dealing with the stresses of raising teenagers. Whenever she felt angry with her son's behaviour, she would take out her frustration by scrubbing the bathtub. Now many years later they maintain a good relationship, however, the enamel is completely worn from the tub.

The Long Distance Runner

You have to question the enjoyment factor for people who run long distance races. If you get the chance, stand at the finish line and watch the faces of the competitors at completion. They will be gaunt, pale faced, and covered in sweat, slobber and potentially other bodily fluids. It looks like a lot of work, and rewarding I am sure. Some of them will no doubt be smiling; I suspect this is because they know the ordeal is over.

Meg's Fave Recipes

Here two of my favourite Recipes that are virtually guaranteed to Boost and Sustain your energy levels.

Cosmic Cookies
– The best protein laden fun snack ever made

Vancouver Island Granola
– Start your day with something sweet and crunchy.

COSMIC COOKIES

Ingredients:

2 ¼ cups	Quick cooking/large flake oats
1 ¾ cups	Dark Chocolate chips
2 cups	Spelt or Whole Wheat Flour
1 ¼ cups	Raisins
1 cup	Sunflower Seeds
¼ cup	Water
¾ cup + 2 tbsp.	Pumpkin Seeds
¼ cup	Blackstrap or fancy molasses
½ cup	Shredded Coconut, unsweetened
¾ cup	Canola oil
¼ cup	Flax Seeds
1 cup	Milk or Soy milk
1 cup	Granulated cane sugar (white sugar)
1	Egg beaten (optional but good to use)
1 tbsp.	Cinnamon, ground
2 ¼ tsp.	Sea salt

Method:
Preheat oven to 350 F. Line baking trays with parchment paper (I've found this to be optional).

In a large bowl, combine dry ingredients, everything from oats to raisins. In a separate bowl combine wet ingredients, everything from water to milk. Add wet ingredients to dry ingredients and mix at a low speed (or by hand) until just combined. Do not over mix.

Portion cooking dough using a 1/3 cup measure (I find using an ice cream scoop with the button release easier) and place on lined baking tray.
Gently flatten cookies before baking.

Bake for approximately 22 minutes, or until lightly browned
Yields 24 cookies.

Meg Soper

VANCOUVER ISLAND GRANOLA

10 cups	Rolled oats
1 cup	Oat bran
1 cup	Powdered skim milk
1 cup	Wheat germ
1 cup	Bran
1 cup	Any chopped nuts (walnuts, sunflower seeds, pumpkin seeds, almonds)
1 cup	Raisins or cranberries (added ½ way through the baking)
1 cup	Honey (liquid)
1 cup	Canola oil

Method:
Preheat oven to 275 F. Heat oil and honey in pot together. Bring to a boil and then remove from heat.

In a large bowl, combine dry ingredients. Mix together. Add oil and honey to ingredients and stir together.

Spread over 4 baking sheets and bake until lightly browned. (Approximately 60 – 90 minutes)

Add raisins/cranberries ½ way through baking to keep from drying out.

Check every 30 min and stir with a fork to ensure even baking

The Ultimate Food Item:
The Liquor Dipped Chocolate Potato Chip…it has just about everything.

"Don't tell your problems to people: eighty percent don't care, and the other twenty percent are glad you have them." – Lou Holtz (Football Coach)

Chapter 7

Nurture the Good Ones – Family and Relationships

Family

I was brought up in an environment where I was expected to do something while I was doing something else. In our home, keeping busy was the ultimate objective. If you weren't officially doing something you had better make it look as if you were, otherwise you risked being assigned an activity you likely didn't care for. If you had a dental appointment you were strongly encouraged to bring along some homework in case you had to wait for 10 minutes. No Reader's Digest or staring into space for me. That ten minutes represented valuable time to improve on my scholastics. As a result, relaxation to this day is somewhat of a challenge and something I plan for.

Also, to say my parents were protective would be a wild understatement. In my early teens other kids were allowed to go out and play after dinner. As for me, I had to have a permission slip signed in triplicate to get to the end of the driveway. But, as we all know, kids are creative. So, as an adventurous teenager, I eventually engineered my own version of the Great Escape, right from my own bedroom window: With one foot on the desk, I could gingerly slide open the window, step down onto the garbage bin, shimmy onto the driveway and hop on my bike. Voila! Social life gamely restored. This procedure met with success for several weeks until one of my older brothers decided to avenge some previous grudge. He locked my window, thus preventing re-entry. I had to take another incognito route through the basement, only to find that he had booby trapped that point of entry by stacking two dozen empty pop cans against the door, which toppled over on my return. Not only were my parents alerted to my nocturnal antics, so was every neighbour within a 500 metre radius. That ensured I was put under surveillance for the balance of the summer.

Moving Slowly Sure Beats Not Moving At All

My mother is 88 years old, and has lived on her own on the east coast of Vancouver Island since my father's passing more than 10 years ago. She continues to be a great source of material for my presentations. "Juners" is quite a vision in her lime green crocks, white long-sleeved shirt and beige 'hand me up' pants that I wore in grade 8. One of her classic lines came when she was in her early 80's and quipped "I move slowly, but at least I'm still moving." When asked at the time if she was going to attend her granddaughter's upcoming wedding she replied, "I'd love to, but I don't know if I'll be alive, so I'm not booking my flight yet."

During any family visit, Mom will make it her mission to clear the freezer of as much food as possible. There is always something she "just has to use up" or the visit won't be considered a success. On one particular visit, the "must use" food item was a rather large salmon. The 15 pound fish was caught by Father Brant, a local historian and friend of Mom's. The fish had been wrapped in a black garbage bag and stored in the freezer for approximately six months before our visit. Mom's method of thawing food was to place it in the oven so the dog couldn't get access to it on the counter top. Of course, it was of some importance to remember not to turn the oven on while the fish was thawing, which was going to be for a considerable time given the size of this particular specimen.

The fish went in the cool oven and people went about their day. All was calm until my daughter decided to make some muffins and turned the oven on to 350 degrees. About 15 minutes later the foul stench of smoldering polyethylene and thawing fish permeated the household. Now any other rational human being would consider this salmon inedible and dispose of it accordingly. Not my mother. It was perfectly fine and there was nothing to get in the way of us enjoying Father Brant's generous offering for dinner that evening. As you might imagine, it was hard to muster much of an appetite knowing of the toxic brew of chemicals that had been infused into the fish. In the interest of family harmony, we choked back a sufficient amount of the spoiled offering to appease my mother, each of us managing a strained smile and choking out an obligatory "gee, pretty tasty fish" in order to qualify for dessert. Even the dog wanted no part of this meal, as she positioned herself on the other side of the room during the dinner proceedings. You know it is bad when a dog refuses cooked salmon.

Relationships
Happiness is an inside job. Accept what you can't change, and take responsibility for what you can.

We celebrate the small successes along the way. After 21 years of marriage, Andy and I have celebrated all kinds of milestones – from our first Christmas together, to moving into our first apartment, to getting a dog, to witnessing the birth of a son and daughter, to outlasting the washer and dryer we got when we moved into our first home (I guess that was why we signed up for the extended warranty – just look where it got us).

This much we know…our time is precious. Being able to distinguish between nurturing relationships versus toxic ones is essential to maintaining our mental health. We know we cannot expect to be able to change other people's behaviour. All we can do is control how we react to that behaviour, and avoid enabling the behaviour that is causing us hurt or concern. It's not about what happens to us… it's about how we react to what happens to us that matters.

In the early days of our marriage I mentally kept track of annoyances… stored them away in a rolodex in my mind so I could call them back in an argument. That didn't work out too well in terms of marital harmony. We now make an effort to keep it in the present. We had to "lose the score card" unless it was for something positive which really carries through in all relationships.

However, if the negative outweighs the positive consistently, then we have to question if the relationship is healthy. Let me share a personal story.

Several years ago I chose to end a friendship that went back more than 30 years. Today I still grieve that loss. I had known this friend (let's call her Sheila) since early high school days and we had always been close. Our paths had both brought us east from Vancouver and we ended up raising our families in the same community. We shared many memorable times together over the years as we raised our families. Then things changed and our friendship became strained. It took several years of conflict with Sheila to realize the relationship wasn't about to change. We would get together and try to resolve things. After, I would drive away with my stomach in knots, a headache, and an overwhelming sense of fatigue. This may have been good for weight loss, but ultimately it was not good for my health.

Distinguishing between a toxic and a nurturing relationship took years for me to realize. We have people in our lives that lift us up emotionally and spiritually, and I believe we need to devote our energy to those relationships. Creating and maintaining quality personal relationships is critical to maintaining our emotional and mental health.

I still work on "letting go" of the thoughts that sometimes work to pull me down. A great deal of energy was spent on trying to fix an unhealthy relationship. I finally realized it was better to "let it go" and to focus on moving forward.

I believe that in a normal, healthy relationship, what you put out you will receive in equal measure. I believe that with all my heart.

What makes for a successful relationship?
In my presentations, I often ask my audiences to volunteer what they feel is the key to the success of their most important relationship... any relationship. The answers are always heartfelt, if not entertaining! Here are a few:

Respect - Communication - Sense of humour - Trust - Saying you're sorry - Two TV sets - Buy a horse (when I heard this I thought they said "get a divorce") - Tolerance - Shift work - Replace the word 'but' with 'and'.

Think Your Good Thoughts Out Loud

Too often, I think we wait until people move away, or leave our lives before we think to tell them how much we appreciate them.

Working in the Operating Room brings home the fact that we derive enjoyment from our work when we work well as a team: when you feel that sense of engagement, when you know you make a difference, and when you are working towards a common goal. Whether it is volunteer work or a career, when you feel that sense of engagement, it is energizing.

I remember one of those day shifts in the operating room where nothing seemed to go right. There were issues with the instruments. The surgeons were annoyed. The cases were delayed and patients were frustrated. It only got worse as the day went on. That afternoon, at home, I received a phone call from one of the senior nurses I had worked with that day. We did not know each other well as she would rarely acknowledge you in the hallway if you passed by her. It was a surprise to hear her voice on the other line. She called to say, "Good job today... we worked well as a team." Wow. What an impact those words made. I remember where I was standing in the kitchen as if it happened yesterday and it was 14 years ago. You never know how far a kind word will go or how it will impact that person at that time.

We have an opportunity every day to inspire the people around us, the people we work with and live with, that we sometimes take for granted.

When Giving Praise ... Don't Wait for a Miracle
Catch them on the little things. Celebrate those small successes along the way. This is meaningful in the workplace and at home. If you get to the end of the day and you can't think of anything, make something up:

> "I love the way your muscles ripple when you take out the garbage!"

> "When you bend down and pick up that garbage can ... my knees buckle."

Get creative. We have the opportunity every day to celebrate the people in our lives, personally and professionally.

> *"Kind words can be short and sweet, but their echoes are endless." - Mother Teresa*

If You Are Going to Squabble, Make sure it is Worth It!
We have had some major arguments throughout our marriage. Most of us do. In retrospect, some were ridiculous. Fortunately, we can look back and laugh. We fought over what type of milk we should feed to our new son; what type of inline roller skates we should purchase for our one year anniversary; and lord knows any number of other trivial things that I cannot remember now. Over the years, I know we have both matured and can more readily gauge if a particular issue is worthy of such energy. In essence, it really does come down to effective communication. Because it's not about who is right or wrong. Being able to really feel it from the other person's point of view makes the difference. We know now, looking

back, that it really did not matter which type of milk we agreed on or how much we spent on the skates... it is the fact we worked through it and can laugh at the memory.

OBSTACLES – Sometimes you do not see them coming.

Obstacles are different to everyone. A number of years ago, I took a trip to Arizona with two of my nursing girlfriends. We had varied interests, but were committed to finding something fun to do while we stayed together. I longed to be next to nature; Cathy was an avid shopper; and Janet wanted to nuzzle in with a good book.

One morning, we set out to fulfill each priority. They dropped me at the foot of Saddleback Mountain and they made their way to Scottsdale Mall. I was armed with a cell phone, a 250 ml bottle of water, a hat, and a granola bar. They were armed and dangerous, with a credit card and a novel. We all thought we had what we needed.

The temperature at 9:00 a.m. was 80 degrees and just starting to warm up. Saddleback Mountain rises several thousand feet above the desert floor, with a marked hiking trail. Fashion Square Mall, located 15 minutes from the drop off has escalators to move you from concourse to mezzanine as you peruse the endless array of shops with marble floors, complete with air conditioning and an inviting coffee bar with cozy couches. We were all set. We agreed to meet back at the drop off location at 12:30 p.m.

On the way up the mountain, I met a woman who suggested I go right up over the top and down the other side. It sounded simple enough: up the hump, along the saddle, up to the summit for a beautiful panoramic view of the city and then down the other side. I took comfort seeing so many hikers along the way and I motored along passing one after the other with a kick in my step. I might have been a tad ambitious. It took just under 90 minutes to get to the parking lot on the other side. Lots of time left to retrace my steps if I kept the same pace, as opposed to walking around the bottom of the mountain, which would be further and oh so boring.

It was at this time, I realized my meagre water supply and lack of sunscreen wasn't going to do wonders for my stamina. There wasn't much I could do about that. Back up I trekked, got to the top of the mountain again, took in the view for one minute then started the final descent.

However, somehow I took the wrong trail. There were no other people on the path; the trail wasn't clearly marked any longer, because I wasn't on one. I kept making my way down until I realized I was stuck. Upon surveying the predicament - I had cactus all around me, combined with unstable rocks and was precariously perched on a steep slope of a rock face. I couldn't retrace my steps without slipping down the side of the mountain. I tried to use my cell phone, but the call would drop. The tears came. I cried out for help. I yelled for help as loud as I could over and over again.

Finally, after about half an hour that seemed like an eternity, I heard a reply. "We can hear you, but we can't see you. Stay where you are". There, far ahead on the horizon, were three intrepid men who emerged from a distant trail and made their way over. They cautiously worked their way down to me. One held out his hand while the other two stabilized his position. They skillfully pulled me up off the rock face. I was hyperventilating ... sobbing ... and panic stricken. They calmed me down, accepted my hug as thanks, and put me back on the proper trail down the mountain.

An hour later I was back at the drop off point, still shaking, emotionally and physically exhausted, yet miraculously right on time for pick up.

Meanwhile, back at the air conditioned, marble-covered mall, Cathy had tried to return some pants she had purchased at the start of their day and they would only give her a store credit. She was battling it out at the checkout, sweat pouring off her brow as she adamantly insisted they should take the pants back and give her the refund. Then, they couldn't remember where they had parked the car, so by the time they found it they were 30 minutes late to pick me up! I had barely escaped falling off the side of a mountain and still made it to the pick-up spot on time.

Cathy was in a state when she picked me up. "You wouldn't believe what I've been through. Talk about stressful."

I took it in, asked for the water bottle and reasoned that we all face stress and obstacles every day and measure them according to our own perspective.

Valuable Lesson:

When you are stuck between a rock and a hard place... be sure to yell for help.

Chapter 8

Random Musings on Life and Your Legacy

Why Life is Complicated & What You Can Do

We have too many passwords to remember. You write the code numbers and pin numbers down and then you can't remember what you wrote it down on. There are days I'm reluctant to turn the computer off in case I can't remember how to log back on.

Life is certainly getting more complicated. But, I believe each of us is in a position to take control and not let an increasingly complicated world take control of us.

Technology is changing every day. It wasn't that long ago we were wandering around with a 'Walkman' the size of a waffle iron. Now everything is so small. The other day I fished a Kit Kat Slim out of my purse and realized I ate my iPod. It was so small I didn't even notice.

Those of us born in the early 1960's grew up having one black and white television set that had, at the most, three stations to choose from. That was it. There was no hope of a program after midnight, just that familiar Indian Head test pattern that would be there on the screen, and the white noise of zero channels. Now, we have stations too numerous to count, on all these different remotes. You need a background in engineering to program the PVR. Thinking about turning on the TV and operating the remote is enough to make me want to have a nap.

And what did we do for kicks back in those days? We played outside. What a concept that was... actually playing outside. If you had a bike, it had one gear. It just went forward. There were no helmets; the only thing we wore for protection was a nylon bathing suit. We were our own self-appointed safety marshals. There were no seatbelts - we bounced around in the back of the station wagon and kept ourselves amused with games like 'eye spy'. The closest we came to an air bag was sitting beside someone who wouldn't stop talking. Now our car talks to us! "Your door is ajar." "Your tire inflation is low." Why can't they report something helpful? For example, "There's a radar trap ahead." or "You've got parsley between your teeth." That information would be useful.

Back in the day, your home phone number consisted of seven digits. The phone itself weighed about the same as a cast iron frying pan and could double as an assault weapon. Some were even permanently tethered to the wall. You rotated the plastic wheel to dial the number and the higher the number the more time you had to block off to actually make the call.

We went from push button phones to the invention of answering machines and home faxes, which seemed so advanced at the time. It wasn't long before we were in a world of instant and constant communication. With email, cell phones, and blackberries... people have to make appointments just so they can make eye contact with each other. We look down and text more than we look up and talk. Then there is the risk that if you don't immediately respond to someone's email or text, they will assume you have been captured by aliens and taken into space and outside your carriers' service area. "Gee... I didn't hear from you right away... it's been three minutes... is everything okay?"

We are expected to determine what is worthy of our time and attention at all times of the day. There are emails from people we don't even know, whose mission it seems is to entice us to open a sinister attachment. Or the familiar and annoying "pass this message on to 15 people you really care about... it will make their day." Nope, not happening, despite the impending threat of what might happen if we break the chain.

We've gotten to the point where we don't have time to talk to people anymore. There are those times, when we call people secretly hoping to just leave a message so we don't actually have to talk to them. It can be so disappointing when they answer the phone. "Oh you're there. I thought you were going to be out. Let me know when you are going to be out and I'll call back then."

The internet has changed our lives in so many ways. We have Facebook and Twitter. My daughter used to bite people when she was angry with them. Now, she has 869 friends on Facebook. I have seven. One of them is my mother. She can't log on. She can't seem to remember her password.

Technology support in our home comes in the form of our adolescent son Will. On occasion, I would be reduced to tears in front of the computer, having given up all hope from sheer frustration. He would come in and press all the right keys, reroute the router, reconfigure the LAN setting... all this from the same person who cannot replace a roll of toilet paper on the holder in the bathroom.

So, what can we do to cope better with an increasingly complicated world? Well, I think awareness is a big part of it. We can sit back and remember that what really matters are the people in our life and the quality of relationships – and not get drawn into the vortex of the wired world, the latest gadgets, and feeling like we always need to be accessible to everyone. It all comes back to the quality of relationships with the people who are important in our life. Find out what grounds you and focus your energies on those things. If you have scheduled a visit or meeting with someone, shut off the communication device and get connected to the conversation.

I say, when it all gets too complicated and you need to check out, you can always take a vacation and be sure to leave the Blackberry and your troubles behind…which leads me to this travel memory.

What to Do When Your Vacation Goes Sideways
My husband was turning 50 and we wanted to do something REALLY special. Having only been to one all-inclusive resort before, we thought we could give it another go. We picked Cuba this time. It had a great price point and given this was at March Break, that helped the financial situation. I was in charge of booking the trip. Research pointed towards the Tryp Resort in Cayo Coco. A family destination resort was the billing. It all sounded promising.

Off we went…2 teenagers, my husband, Andy and I. An indicator of the adventure that lay ahead unfolded at the airport waiting lounge, as we were surrounded by hyper teenagers whooping it up, before we even boarded the flight to Cuba. Surely they were destined for another resort we mused. I overheard conversations on the flight like, "I brought extra nose rings, because you never know if you're going to get hit in the face with a wave and they might fall out." YIKES. We arrived at our tropical paradise at the same time as 1200 un-chaperoned, unsupervised grade 12 students, unleashed from home for the very first time with open access to free alcohol 24 hours a day. It was completely out of control. I had conjured up visions of doing Pilates and yoga by the pool. Well, you couldn't access any of the facilities as they were overrun with inebriated teenagers. As we walked around the resort we witnessed unruly behaviour of all kinds. Foul language permeated the air around us. We heard words I didn't know existed. Every morning at breakfast a different kid would appear sporting a new injury. One morning a young man wheeled his way in wearing a partial body cast.

Bear in mind, I make a living speaking to audiences about dealing with stressful situations and always looking for the humour. I also facilitate full-day workshops emphasizing teamwork and looking for the best in people. So, for five long arduous days I sucked it up. But then, I couldn't take it any longer.

On Day 5, I was sitting in the Lobby Bar having a cocktail before dinner while writing in my journal. My husband Andy was at the bar getting more drinks for me... he could barely keep up with the demand. Behind me was a table for four, which had morphed to a table of 20 of these kids, and the language was so loud and foul, something inside of me... snapped. I think my blood pressure must have been 200/120 and I felt I was close to having a stroke.

I stood up to address these kids with as much composure as I could muster and said, "You are not in a bubble. There are other people here at this resort, who are

89

trying to enjoy their holiday. If you could just watch your language and keep your voices down a touch that would be really terrific... because I am feeling really angry right now!"

There was a young woman seated directly in front of me with a revealing halter top that exposed more than it contained. She had piercings and staples through numerous body parts. She was giving her gum an invigorating workout while she looked entirely bored with my comments. She glanced up at me and as I turned away, the words that emerged from her mouth seemed to stick to the back of my neck. She said, "Why don't you take a ride on the bitter bus?"

I was incredulous, "WHAT? Why don't you take a ride on the bitter bus?" At this point I'm thinking, my bitter bus is fuelled-up and ready to go... why don't you get under it and we can roll on with the day.

Now, I didn't say that, but it certainly helped to think it. I knew I had two choices. I could choose to let those words tip me over the edge, which ultimately could result in a stroke, which might ruin the holiday, OR I could chisel the words off the back of my neck and look for the humour.

So, now I am taking the "Bitter Bus" and "Staple Woman" on the road with me for the rest of my days on earth because it's funny. And, if you can laugh at it... you can survive it. I have actually added "Staple Woman" to my friends on Facebook. She's my seventh friend. I can find out where she is going on vacation and promptly set off in the opposite direction.

No matter what your job title is or what position you hold, if you have the ability to step back from a situation and see the humour in it, you will realize that humour melts stress. Life can be less stressful. Shift your perspective and look for the humour. We were all born with a sense of humour... it is how we choose to use that gift that can make a difference.

What will your legacy be?
If you were told you had five years to live, what would you need to get done? What would be on your bucket list? When you ask yourself this question... what do you come up with?

Do you seriously want to make a change in your life? If you do, then tell someone about it. Write it down. Be accountable. You increase your chances of accomplishing a goal just by telling someone about it. Your chances increase further, when you write the goal down. Create that vision of what you want to achieve. A goal without a vision is like doing a jigsaw puzzle without a picture on the box. How do you know where to start? How do you know how close you are towards your goal without a vision?

During presentations I have heard many answers to this question... Here are a few:

A man in Saskatchewan said, "I need to tell the people in my life I love them. So, I have been doing just that. The other day, I was driving with my 17-year-old daughter when I looked at her and said 'Alyssa I love you.' She just looked back at me and replied, 'Dad, that is so random'."

One woman in Timmins, Ontario said, "I'm going to get in shape so I look good in the casket."

A woman in Scarborough said, "I'm going to eat whatever I want."

A woman from Wallaceburg, Ontario said, "I am going to sit my two girls down, and say, '**Find your brother**'. They don't have one; I just want to mess with their minds."

How do you want to be remembered?
Accept yourself for who you are in this moment, and now accept who you can become. If the way you are living your life does not match up with the way you want to be remembered, accept that fact. Ask yourself what you could do to be living your legacy. Is there anything you want to change or improve to become more in balance? It's never too late to balance your life.

> *"You don't get to choose how you are going to die...or when. You only decide how you're going to live right now."*
> *- Joan Baez*

Balance
It is a challenge, a fine art of keeping all the balls in the air while maintaining a sense of balance. Let's face it; I think many of us have had one of those days when you felt like you might just lose it completely. These six steps have helped me keep it together, because we never know what will come our way.

Meg's 6 Steps to Keep in Balance

1. Remember it is just called life.
2. Stuff happens and you deal with it.
3. Take the time to make the right choices - it usually works out well.
4. If not go to line 2 ...
5. It helps to have good luck, good intentions, timing and some prayer.
6. Mix all the steps together and keep smiling.

We all have an opportunity to reach our potential while maintaining a balanced and fulfilling life. If you don't feel absolutely sure of your abilities, carry on as though you do. You will eventually teach yourself the habit of confidence, which once in place, will take you to places you never imagined!

Listen to your inner spirit. It will guide you, and show you the way through your own experiences. Know that you deserve the best that life has to offer.

> *"We must do the things we cannot do. The future belongs to those who believe in the beauty of their dreams."*
> *- Eleanor Roosevelt*

*"I couldn't wait for success, so I went ahead
without it."* – *Jonathan Winters*

PART III

By Judy Croon

About the Author:

Judy is a comedienne, motivational humourist, MC, radio broadcaster and fundraiser.

Her comedy specials have appeared on CBS, NBC, The Comedy Channel, The Comedy Network, CTV and CBC.

Judy has co-hosted successful morning shows on Toronto's Mix 99.9, LA's KFRG and XM radio.

She is the host and creator of Laughlines and Stand Up for the Girls. Both events so far, have helped raise over $650,000 for breast cancer research.
In Judy's keynotes, she draws from her hilarious experiences on stage and in radio to give audiences techniques to deal with difficult people, stressful lives, tough stains and hard to reach places.

Judy is especially proud to mention that she has never been arrested.

www.JudyCroonSpeaks.com

Judy Croon

INTRODUCTION

I seem to run into two kinds of people: the people who have great luck, but always complain; and the people who have terrible luck, but never complain.

The people who always complain are draining, and the people who never complain are inspiring. Am I complaining too much about the people who complain?

We all have bad luck sometimes, but I think our courage to persevere comes from a number of sources including hope, faith and many times, humour.

My humour comes from my parents. My dad is from Holland. My mom is from Guyana. I'm actually half Dutch, one-quarter Asian, one-eighth black and one-eighth vodka.

My mother is a character. She's direct and brutally honest. My two sisters and I always joke that if you want information from someone, don't send in the CIA or the KGB - send in my mother. She's also the first person to poke fun at herself.

My dad on the other hand is funny, but in a "Dutch" way. He's quirky. He says things in a very matter-of-fact manner. People either laugh nervously, because they're not sure if he's serious, or because they're afraid of his 6 foot 4, 250-pound, imposing figure.

From both of them, my two sisters and I grew up learning the art and importance of humour. Humour has a way of cocooning us when, as Jack Nicholson says in *A Few Good Men*, "You can't handle the truth!"

People like Jon Stewart, Stephen Colbert and Tina Fey remind us every day to roll with the punches of an ever-changing, challenging world.

Me? Shrugging my shoulders like Tony Soprano, I can't complain. My life has not been perfect. Mistakes – Oh, I've made a few! Some I'll even admit to-like Nortel. But every day, I laugh (sometimes at inappropriate times), I learn and I slowly, methodically move on.

I am forever grateful to my parents for the lessons that they taught my sisters and me, in life. I'm especially grateful to my mother for a lesson that I hope I can pass onto others.

If you can't laugh at yourself, I'll show you how.

Judy Croon

Chapter 9

To Hell Gigs and Back
- Lessons From the Road

"We all have big changes in our lives that are more or less a second chance." Harrison Ford

Where do comics come from?
People always wonder what comedians are like when they're kids - that we all have a dark past. Not true. I had a great life growing up. That's not to say that I wasn't a bit of a weird kid. I grew up with two sisters. I was the oldest. Whenever they asked me to play, I'd have to control the game and it would always turn into a Steven Spielberg production.

If we were playing Barbies; Barbie's beach bus would drive off the road, get a flat tire; Ken would go for help; Barbie would get her leg caught underneath a log; Dawn would have to amputate Barbie's leg; Barbie would die of infection; Ken would lose his eyesight and be stuck on the edge of a cliff; etc, etc.

I was always singing and dancing. I was Gladys Knight. My sisters were the Pips. I was always coming up with money-making schemes. I made my first ten dollars in grade two painting and selling rocks to my classmates.

99

I always wanted to save animals. I formed a club. We met in my garage. I was the president. Everyone in the group had to write a report on an animal. God bless Sheila Stewart. She was the only one who submitted a paper on porcupines. The rest of my friends gave me the finger and took off on their bikes.

I was a bit of a nerd. At least, I was a funny nerd. In grade eight, I came in second in the Catholic District School Board Speech Competition of Toronto. I still can't believe that my *'History of Puns'* came in second to Steve Ireland's *'Who Really Killed JFK?'* How tired is that topic? Puns - I was ahead of my time.

The Outsider

Yes, folks are always curious how comedians can stand on stage and face the fear of a judging crowd. I think it might partially have to do with an 'outsider' complex. Comedians are always on the outside looking in - observing. Sometimes, we are placed there because we don't 'fit in'. In my case, I had a great childhood, but I was a *bit* eccentric. Painted rocks and a funeral for Barbie? C'mon – I was used to people sometimes looking at me differently.

15 Minutes

I always wanted to do something BIG. Unfortunately, I was always bit of a chicken. So, whatever I did, I would do in small, methodical steps in what started out as fifteen minutes a day. For me, fifteen minutes a day was the only thing that stood between me and my BIG plans to take over the world - whether it was becoming a veterinarian or a comedienne or an Olympic Volleyball champion or a sitcom actress or a pop star or a Bay Street Investor, etc. etc.!

Lord of the Flies

I never thought I would be a stand-up comedienne. As a teen, I wore blinders. I wanted to be a veterinarian. I studied with that in mind. I even worked at a veterinarian's office for three years.

Slowly, over time, however I made a realization. You practically have to be more educated than a paediatric neurosurgeon to get into vet school. Then after receiving your Nobel Prize in Biochemistry, you spend a lot of time doing neuters and spays.

This is when I felt really bad for the cats and dogs that came into our office. They would come into the waiting room and see the other dogs and cats and think, "Oh good, a party!" Then, we'd give them drugs and tie them down. Now they were thinking, "Kinky!" Next thing, they would wake up with a lampshade on their head and more than just their car keys missing. I couldn't do it.

On top of this revelation, I had a science experiment that went REALLY wrong. One fateful day, at the University of Calgary, six generations of fruit flies and 75% of my final mark flew out of the biology class window. I walked off that campus - never to return again.

That night, I went home in a daze. I turned on the TV. It was the Tonight Show with Johnny Carson. A woman named Joan Rivers was telling jokes. That's when I had my a-ha moment- as 'Queen Oprah' would call it. I would do stand–up comedy. What a natural transition from wanting to be a veterinarian - NOT. What the hell was I thinking? At the very least, I could dedicate fifteen minutes a day to this idea until I came up with a better plan.

So, where does one learn to do stand-up comedy? Calgary, of course! Despite the fact that I had never even taken a drama class in high school, I thought, how hard could it be?

Now that I look back on it, when those fruit flies flew out that biology class window, I must have had a complete mental breakdown. I must have inhaled too much ether. What compelled me to think that I could be funny, much less that I could write five minutes of funny material without any previous comedy writing experience and perform it in front of a room full of strangers???

Needless to say, the week leading up to my first five-minute performance was sheer hell. I became more terrified each passing day. I couldn't eat, I couldn't sleep. What if I forgot my material???

Is This On?
The moment just before I was supposed to perform, I remember standing backstage. I was so scared that I thought I was going to pass out. Just then, the MC

introduced me. As my name was leaving his lips, I still contemplated bolting for the back door. But, I didn't. Instead my lead-filled legs walked me out onto that smoke-filled stage in Calgary. (Those were the days when everybody still smoked - especially in comedy clubs.) I walked up to the microphone. The audience waited in anticipation. It was like a spaghetti western. I looked at the audience. The audience looked at me. I looked at the MC. The MC looked at the audience.

I was so paranoid that I was going to forget my material that I practiced it at least a thousand times into a hairbrush before I actually performed it. Thank goodness. I sailed through my material effortlessly. I did not forget a word or a beat or a gesture. There was only one minor detail; I forgot to make it funny. People stared at me for what felt like an eternity. It was as if the minute hand on a clock was ticking backwards. TICK TICK TICK. Finally, when the water boarding torture was over for the audience *and* me, I left the stage to a warm round of *applaud*. I still don't remember driving home.

Back To the Drawing Board
As bad as I was, it didn't faze me. I kept driving to that club, 45 minutes from my house for the next year, once a week, for free, slowly working on my set, fifteen minutes at a time and honing my craft. I kept writing, I kept performing and I kept experimenting on stage.

Sure, there were a million times that I wanted to quit. Every time I had a bad set, I initially wanted to throw in the towel, but then the next day, I would start thinking about what I could do differently to make the set better the next time.

> *"When your dreams turn to dust; vacuum."*
> *~ Author Unknown*

Think About the Money - Chump Change and Chimp Suits

Over the first year of stand-up, I got my first 15 minute set together, which turned into 30 minutes (2 fifteen minute sets in my mind). I was ready to hit the road. I wasn't exactly ready for The Tonight Show, but I could certainly earn some money being an MC and an opening act.

However, this was Alberta in its comedy infancy. There weren't exactly a ton of plum one-nighters to pick from. Luckily, I didn't know the difference and ventured on naively.

> *"I played one club...it was so far out, my act was reviewed in Field and Stream."* - Rodney Dangerfield

I remember one of the first paying gigs that I ever did was for an all-female audience at a male 'exotic' night club - if you get my drift. It was a bachelorette party and the last things those girls wanted to see was another woman standing on stage, telling jokes for half an hour. The management was smart; they paid me my money for the show, up front. So as I was standing on stage, dying the death of a thousand screams, all I could hear was, "Boo, bring on the male exotic dancers."

All I could think about was the money burning a hole in my pocket. Two minutes, five minutes, fifteen minutes, twenty minutes... just when I thought things couldn't get any worse, at the twenty–eight minute mark, all hell broke loose. One of the male exotic dancers had a monkey on a leash (don't ask). They were standing in the back of the room. As I was launching into one of my last jokes, the monkey on the leash got away from his owner and started charging towards the stage. I let out a blood-curdling scream. To heck with it, I was going to run. Just then, the audience broke into a big roar of laugher. I took a bow, said, "Thank you", and quickly, exited the stage. I got my money, they got their laugh, I was out of there. That's when I learned a big life lesson. **When all else fails, keep your sense of humour and think about the money!**

"Drive on. We'll sweep up the blood later."- Katherine Hepburn

The '-40 Below Tour' with Dionne Warwick

I continued slowly putting my act together joke by joke, bit by bit, 30 minutes, 45 minutes (three fifteen minutes!), then, an hour (four fifteen minutes). I drove all over Western Canada and performed at any one-nighter that would hire me. I got the names and numbers of agents and bookers from the American comics that I worked with in Calgary. I packed up my car and toured the Northeast US for three months by myself. It's only years later that my

Mom told me she didn't sleep a wink the whole time that I was gone because she was so worried. I probably would have felt the same if my daughter packed up her car to do stand-up comedy! But, it was the weirdest thing, I JUST HAD to do it. I just had to know.

Something was driving me forward and I just couldn't explain what it was. Through my experiences in comedy, I did get to work with some celebrities: comedian Robert Klein, Weird Al, Anne Murray, country sensation Wynonna, but one of my strangest, yet most memorable early celebrity encounters happened when I worked with 60's/70's icon Dionne Warwick (waaaay before her 'Celebrity Apprentice' days).

I was hired to open for Dionne in five theatres across Western Canada. Promoters nicknamed it, "The - 40 Below Tour." The tour included; Calgary, Edmonton, Winnipeg, Regina and Saskatoon. My parents were big fans of Dionne Warwick so I vowed to make them proud.

I couldn't wait to meet her. I was opening for my first celebrity! When I entered the back of the auditorium of our first venue in Calgary - my eyes darted around, looking for the star. I didn't see her. Another twenty minutes went by. Then I walked by Dionne's green room. The door was open. I couldn't believe it. I heard the sound of a Ms Pacman video game. As I slowly passed by, I saw 60s/70s icon Dionne Warwick, hunched over an actual arcade-sized Ms. Pacman machine. It had all the bells and whistles. In one hand, Dionne held the joystick to Ms.

Pacman, and in the other hand she held a long cigarette. She took uninterrupted drags of her cigarette as her eyes remained transfixed on the screen.

I asked the tour manager what the deal was. He said Dionne had it in her contract that in every venue she was to perform at on the tour, she needed to have an arcade-sized Ms. Pacman game in her green room. I would be lying if I didn't say, in that moment, I felt slightly jealous. Yes, I had so much to be grateful for in my life, but this was Ms. Pacman!

A Class Canadian Act-Anne Murray

Then there was my encounter with Canadian icon, Anne Murray. At this point, I was now working full-time doing stand-up in the Northeast United States. I was hired to open for Ms. Murray in Connecticut and New Jersey.

I was backstage at the theatre in Connecticut, looking for my Green Room. Suddenly, Anne Murray popped out of her Green Room and warmly extended her hand. She said, "Hi, I'm Anne." How humble. How nice. How normal. How Canadian.

Then she apologized for the smell of cigar smoke. She said she would smoke a cigar to warm up her voice. Go figure - Anne Murray - The Frank Sinatra of Canadian Show Business. Love it. She was so down to earth. Then again, what else would you expect from someone from the Maritimes? Anne was awesome!

"Humility is greatness in plain clothes" - Spencer W. Kimball

Full Circle - Yes, We Can Talk

Dionne was eccentric, Anne was awesome, but the celebrity encounter that really brought my life full circle happened early this year - 2011.

I got a call to open for Joan Rivers at Roy Thomson Hall. Would I open for and then interview Joan on stage afterwards? I couldn't believe my ears.

I met Joan before the show. She was quiet, but very sweet. Everybody asks me what she looks like close up? Well yes, she looked like she's had work done, but she's also seventy-eight years old!

I went on stage first. The audience was great. They were in a fabulous mood. Then I had to introduce Joan. Whereas most comics want you to introduce them with 80 credits, Joan Rivers who has 8000 credits basically said, "Aw heck, just bring me up." Joan Rivers took the stage and the audience loved her. She was up there for fifty minutes. It was an assortment of signature machine-gun-one-liners combined with some very funny and very sad stories about her life (most of which are covered in her edgy documentary *A Piece of Work*). I highly recommend the film.

After Joan finished her set, I joined her on stage and we talked for thirty minutes. I had nothing to worry about; she was warm, humble, engaging and hilarious. She had some terrific stories. For example, Joan said she was a friend of Camilla and Charles. In fact, she has a crush on

Charles. She says he's funny, charming and still holds a door open for a lady. Joan says if she could have actively pursued Charles back in the day, Camilla wouldn't have stood a chance!

At one point, I asked Joan what's the first thing that she bought when she knew she 'made it.' That was after her debut on the Tonight Show when Johnny Carson looked over at her and said, "You're going to be a big star." She said she bought herself a mink coat. Don't tell Greenpeace!

My evening with Joan Rivers was amazing. Those 2500 people at Roy Thomson Hall were suddenly 2500 friends sitting in our living room. All those smoky clubs, snow-filled highways and Norman Bates motels of the past now seemed to make sense. I had my 2 x 15 minutes of fame with Joan. 15 minutes - that's all you need to change your life!

"We did not change as we grew older; we just became more clearly ourselves." - Lynn Hall

*"How people treat you is their karma;
how you react is yours."* **Wayne Dyer**

Judy Croon

Chapter 10
Rubber Chicken Soup
- Hecklers and Stage Fright

Radio: Chicken Wings, Bed Races and Demolition Derbies

I continued doing stand-up comedy for the next ten years, making my living across Canada. At some point though, I decided that I probably wouldn't want to be on the road for the rest of my life. What was I going to do? Radio had always intrigued me. I decided to pursue it - fifteen minutes at a time.

I was able to get a job at a brand new radio station in Ottawa. I had very little 'on-air' experience, so I started on the overnight show - the 'Grooveyard shift'. Within a year, I had worked my way up to co-hosting the morning show. I never got used to getting up at three-thirty in the morning.

Have a Master Plan
One particular time, I remember waking up from a foggy afternoon nap, only to have to drive downtown to taste 10 different types of chicken wings and ribs for a chicken and ribs festival. It was 30 degrees outside. I wanted to pass out.

One time, in the middle of winter, I was being pushed in a bed going 30 km/hour down the middle of Rideau Street for a charity bed race. I wanted to sleep.

Another time, I was competing in a Demolition Derby for a radio station in LA. The old Cadillac I was driving got t-boned just as another car caught on fire. I wanted to die.

When I got the morning show in Ottawa, I decided that the only way that I was going to get through it was to *have a master plan*. The people of Ottawa couldn't be nicer, but the pressure of that new show was intense. I knew I was going to leave after three years. I circled the date on my calendar. I followed my number one rule: I maintained my sense of humour and I thought about the money!

Michael Bolton
We did have some fun times. Like the afternoon that our radio station played Michael Bolton's softball team for a celebrity charity event. We thought it was going to be really casual. Michael Bolton was in town for a concert and we were going to have a 'fun' game with proceeds going to charity. Our ragtag team arrived at the baseball diamond. Rumour has it that Michael Bolton's team included some ex-professional players! They killed us with a score of something like 36-2. I think I got on base once. Oh, we can laugh now.

Celine Dion
Then there was the time that I took winners backstage to meet Celine Dion. She was amazing. She couldn't be more

gracious if she tried. She took her time and spoke to each winner without rushing them. Class act - Canadian eh?

Use What You Have

Three years to the date that I started the morning show in Ottawa, I handed in my resignation. I got my work visa and moved to the States. I had friends in New York, and so I decided to move there and use it as a base. Over the next three years, I worked the clubs in New York, New Jersey, Pennsylvania, Washington DC, West Virginia and pretty well, anywhere in between. I also picked up the occasional radio gig in New York, so I didn't have to be on the road as much.

After three years of stand-up on the East Coast, I moved to the West Coast. I moved to Los Angeles for another three years where I picked up another radio gig.

What I learned over those six years in the US not only taught me a lot about comedy and radio, it taught me a lot about life. It taught me how to write, it taught me how to create and survive, and it taught me how to deal with hecklers no matter what kind of situation I was in. It taught me to use the skills that I had and it drove me to discover the skills that I needed. It didn't fix my whiplash from the demolition derby though.

Taming Hecklers - Dealing With Difficult People
"Courage is grace under pressure." Ernest Hemingway

In showbiz, a heckler is a person in the audience who disrupts the show. In business, a heckler is the person who disrupts the flow.

As a performer, I noticed that there were three specific types of hecklers in an audience; the bullies, the snipers and the Homer Simpson Incompetents (The people who make noise, but don't know what they really want).

In my experience working with business clients, I've noticed there is a one-to-one co-relation with hecklers in the club and hecklers in the workplace (co-workers and customers).

General Heckler Management Tips
The first thing you learn as a comedian is to always maintain control of the room - no matter what is going on. You have to claim your space on stage. You have to be the leader, the alpha dog. Worse than a heckler ruining one joke is a heckler ruining your entire act because you let them get to you. Stay in control. Stay confident. Don't panic.

As comedienne Elaine Boosler use to say in the deodorant ads (I love Elaine because she's got the word 'booze' right in her name), "Never let them see you sweat."

The audience always looks at the heckler first to see who it is that said something stupid, then they look at the stage to see how the comic is going to react. You, not the heckler, control the REACTION of the room.

The pack is looking at the alpha dog to take their cue.

Next, whether you're dealing with a bully, a sniper or a Homer Simpson drunk, remember to walk lightly, but carry a big schtick. You're confident right???? You've got control of the situation right???

Dealing with a heckler incorrectly makes you the goat. Dealing with a heckler correctly makes you the rock star. Don't panic. Stay calm. Take your time and plan your approach.

Walk Lightly, But Carry A Big Schtick
If someone in the audience says something, I tend to initially let it go. I give the person the benefit of the doubt. They might just be ordering a drink. It's usually harmless and not worth stopping the show for everyone else.

If I maintain my professionalism and look like I'm cool-headed, then I will continue to have the support of my other co-workers (in my case, the audience)

On the one hand, if I immediately go for the heckler's jugular vein and attack his mother and six generations before that, then I will suddenly look like the jerk.

So initially, I choose to ignore the heckler. However, if the heckling continues, then I have to single out the heckler. I will slowly ramp up my interactions with them, hoping that I solve the problem early and as effortlessly as possible. I'm letting them know that I'm aware of them, but I'm not stopping the flow of the show.

In a work environment, you single out your heckler by setting up a time to see them privately. As in the club, this lets your 'heckler' know that you are aware of them. More importantly, like a comic taking note of when and where a heckler can re-appear from the weeds, you mentally take note of everything that happens in your meeting and then document it afterwards.

Did you know that it takes the average worker, who is having problems at work, one and a half years to complain to upper management? Do you honestly think you can remember everything that happened over eighteen months ago? Write it down.

Maintain Your Poise

Do not raise your voice. Do not let the heckler get to you. I heard a great story about a kindergarten teacher who had 'the class from hell' according to other teachers. However, she personally never had any problems with those students? Why? Because every morning she walked into that classroom like she was Clint Eastwood. In all those westerns and Dirty Harry Movies, Clint barely speaks beyond a whisper and how scary is Clint Eastwood? There have been times that I've been intimidated by an audience (i.e. Staten Island); I put on my poncho and got on stage. Whether it's on stage, in the boardroom or in the classroom, just remember, even if you don't feel confident, act confident.

Ask For Help

If going forward with your heckler, go to your boss or HR department and ask for help. Show your notes from your private meetings. Worst case scenario, what if your heckler from hell is your boss? To that I say, "Maintain your sense of humour and think about the money!"

I was once working at a radio station with someone who I did not get along with, for years. I complained to management a number of times, but nobody wanted to rock the boat. So every day, I just thought about the money I was making until I found an opportunity to get out!

It's Not You

Remember, above all, ninety-nine percent of the time - it's not you. I can't tell you how many times a heckler has walked up to me after the show and said, "Hey, WE were great. That was funny." Sure buddy, like WE'RE taking this gig on the road together. Comedy club and workplace hecklers are sometimes, completely oblivious to their own behaviour.

Schoolyard Bullies

Sadly, bullying has not only become too common in workplaces, it is also in schools across North America. Ultimately, if schoolyard bullies aren't dealt with, they grow up to become workplace bullies. There were bullies at my school when I was growing up and occasionally, I was the target of their assaults. Not fun.

At least, back in my day (the Crimean era) the internet wasn't around. Cyber-bullying is now a 24 hour/7 day a week issue. Norway seems to have programs in their schools and workplaces that might be worth implementing into our systems. The Norwegian Project was developed out of a government 'manifesto' in 2002 that stated that bullying in Norwegian schools would be reduced to 0% in three years. A tall order, for sure, but bullying is down to 50% in some of their schools. The Norwegian Project is based on three principles:

- Zero Tolerance

- Everyone (including parents) is encouraged to report any incidences of bullying to the school whether those incidences occur on or off school property.

- Integration of anti-bullying methods into the general education and weekly school curriculum (teachers start their day asking students if there are any issues they need to talk about).

If you are interested in this program, I encourage you to watch this fascinating documentary:

http://archive.teachfind.com/ttv/www.teachers.tv/videos/norway-anti-bullying.html

Mobbing In the Workplace
Workplace bullying is called 'mobbing in the workplace' in Norway.
- As late as the 80's, complaining about bullying in the workplace was considered taboo.

- In the 90's, the Labour Union officials claimed that bullying was the most severe work environment problem and pushed to revise The Norwegian Work Environment Act in 1993.

Zero tolerance, training and education are the foundations of this act, as well. Norwegians take pride in being known as peacemakers. Perhaps we should take a closer look at their programs.

From Schoolyard Bullies to Workplace Bullies
Hecklers are not fun in comedy clubs. Hecklers are not fun in the workplace - whether they are co-workers or clients. Hecklers in schools, however, should especially not be tolerated. Children are our most precious resource. We should do everything to protect them.

Fright Night-Overcoming Stage Fright
Aside from dealing with hecklers, comedy also provides a means of learning how to deal with stage fright. I apply these rules to stand–up; they can also be applied to any presentation.

> *"I learned that courage was not the absence of fear, but the triumph over it. The brave man is not he who does not feel afraid, but he who conquers that fear." - Nelson Mandela*

One of the most common fears is standing in front of a crowd and having to speak. Worse than standing in front of a crowd, is standing in front of a crowd and not knowing what to say. How many times have you had that nightmare?

Practice, practice, practice.
Know your material like the back of your hand. Worst case scenario, you can go on automatic pilot and the audience won't know the difference. Even if you are bombing, it will be quick and painless and you'll appear more confident than you feel. If you don't know your material, it will seem twice as long to you and your audience. Yes, there are comics who improvise on stage as they go along, but typically these are people who have been at it for a while. Why make it so hard on yourself?

Confidence Is Contagious
Knowing your material and being confident, can take you a long way. Confidence is contagious. Audiences like confident comics. Mediocre comics have been given sitcom development deals because they were confident and audiences liked them. Studios can always hire writers. Nobody pays their money to go to a comedy show to feel uncomfortable.

The B Word - Bombing
Even if you're bombing - appear confident. There's nothing funnier than a comic admitting that the show isn't going well and joking about it. It eliminates the elephant in

the room and it shows that you're not taking comedy too SERIOUSLY.

Be Credible

Be yourself. Be credible. Don't do characters, accents, old jokes or take on false emotions (anger, craziness, paranoia, or deadpan delivery) if that's not you. The audience will smell a fake.

Don't Overload

Don't try too much new material at once. You run the risk of it not working and not getting booked again. Stage time is too valuable to blow it. Always, start off strong and end strong. You don't know how a new bit is going to work, so stick it in the middle somewhere.

Oops, I Forgot

What if you're worst fear is realized? You forget your act! You can do one of two things. You can pause or you can admit it. Take a sip of water. Remain calm. Think. Survey the room. A pause never looks as big as it feels. Finally, when all else fails, ask your audience, "What were we talking about?" Confidence is king. Remember, if you're comfortable-your audience is comfortable.

Hell Gig

What if you're at a hell gig and you can't do anything to win the audience over? Do your time and get off the stage. Say, "Thank you and goodnight." It's comedy, not a heart transplant. You died on stage. Nobody died in real life. There's always tomorrow and the reality is there will always be hell gigs. Some of the worst hell gigs stick around the longest on the circuit so get use to it. Remember practice, practice and practice.

Where to Start

How do you get stage time? If you want to try stand-up comedy, do an internet search or call up your local comedy club or local pub. Ask them if they have an amateur night. Many pubs and bars have a comedy night once a week or once a month, because it's free easy entertainment. All the club needs is a microphone and a spotlight. It's not like they have to set up for Earth, Wind and Fire. The crowd and/or the venue may not be great. It won't be The Tonight Show or Late Night with David Letterman, but it will be a great way to find out if you really want to pursue stand-up comedy.

Again, practice, practice and practice,

Above all, remember the number one rule.

WHEN ALL ELSE FAILS, MAINTAIN YOUR SENSE OF HUMOUR AND THINK ABOUT THE MONEY!

Chapter 11

Punch Lines on Purpose - Why Giving Makes Good Business Sense

"You've got to jump off cliffs, all the time and build your wings on the way down." - Ray Bradbury

Fifteen Minutes Re-Visited

The day the fruit flies escaped from me in the lab at university was probably one of the most tumultuous days in my life. I thought that I was going to be a veterinarian. I didn't even consider wanting to be a doctor. I didn't want to help people. I just wanted to help animals. I just wanted to be a vet.

I studied hard. I worked at a veterinarian's office for three years. My plan was sailing along. Then suddenly, with one untimely incident, not only was my rudder taken away, there was also a hole in the boat. I was drowning. Now, what was I going to do with my life?

The night I decided to do stand-up comedy after seeing Joan Rivers on The Tonight Show was certainly one of the strangest decisions I've ever made. However, I planned my approach like it was a new science experiment. I was going to be slow, methodical and consistent in this next phase of my life. If I chipped away at it, in small increments each day, it might not seem so scary. If I didn't look up, I wouldn't see the mountain. Many days my fifteen minute

123

'chunks' turned into much longer periods of time, yet my fifteen minutes got me to the table each and every time.

The Mountain

Over the years, I applied my fifteen minute approach to other career opportunities that comedy opened the door to - radio, fundraising and keynote speaking.

I thought my calling in life was to help animals. I ended up helping people more than I expected.

The next day after my fruit fly experiment and stand-up comedy epiphany, I got to work on my fifteen minute plan. I watched comics on The Tonight Show and Late Night with David Letterman. Some of my favourites at the time were Jerry Seinfeld, Gary Shandling, Richard Lewis, Richard Jeni, Ellen Degeneres, Rosanne Barr, and Louis Anderson.

I read books about stand-up comedy. Then I wrote, practiced, found a club, did a five-minute set (at 'The Brass Cat' in Calgary. Boy, even the name sounds hilarious, doesn't it?). That five-minute set turned into my first fifteen-minute set. I wrote more material, did longer sets, found a booking agent and drove to LA to sample the 'big time'. Then I moved to Toronto to do stand-up comedy full-time. Then I got my visa and moved to the United States. I did my comedy on TV shows in Canada and the US. Eventually, I turned my stand-up comedy into two other professions as well - radio and keynote speaking.

Dedicating fifteen minutes a day to a new passion did two things for me.
   a) It kept me moving forward, albeit, ever so slowly
   b) It kept my passion fresh. Every day I was surprised by something new.

Radio Daze

Along with stand-up comedy, I also learned that I had a passion for radio. It was probably fed by all those thousands of miles driving alone, listening to the radio. Slowly, but surely, I started mapping out a plan of how I was going to cut my way on to the competitive radio circuit. I listened to some of my favourite radio personalities, I read trade magazines. I spoke to people in the business. I investigated courses that were available. I completed a Radio Broadcasting program at Humber, and worked at the radio gig in Ottawa for three years.

LA – The Big One

My passion for radio and comedy took me to New York and Los Angeles. Over the next six years I could be heard on stations like WABC, WALK FM, KCLU, KCRW and KFRG. I loved living in Los Angeles, but I was always freaked out by the fear of a big earthquake.

One particular tremor, I woke up at 4 o'clock in the morning. My building was shaking back and forth. I ran out into the street. I passed a woman calmly standing in her doorway holding a baby. She said, "Are you Canadian?" There were only two other people standing there - both

Canadian. Californians were just too laid back about the quakes!

911

I had always earmarked June 2001 as the approximate time that I would move back to Canada. Lo and behold, I was offered a job in Toronto just around that time at Mix 99.9. I was going to be a news anchor/sidekick on Carla and Company.

I don't know why I picked that time to move back to Canada. However, when I was watching a small TV in our Mix 99.9 studio, and I saw that first airplane crash into the World Trade Centre in New York three months later on September 11, I knew that I would never be moving back to the States.

Donuts and Angels on the Dashboard

It wasn't an earthquake; however, I did have a close call in LA. Luckily, I had a guardian angel looking out for me. (Still today, I feel like it's my great-grandmother, Louissa.)

It happened on a Saturday afternoon. I was cruising southbound 60 mph on the 405 towards Santa Monica, to hook up with some friends. It was a pretty normal, busy drive on the 405, until I looked in the rear-view mirror and I saw a green SUV haphazardly darting in and out of the lanes behind me. Before I knew it, the green SUV was to the left of me. Before I had time to react, he clipped the left quarter panel of my car and spun me around. Everything really does slow down when you think you're about to die!

I remember sitting in the car, and as I did a 360' and then some, I closed my eyes and braced for the impact of another a car certainly t-boning my Honda Civic. Nothing happened. I slowly opened my eyes. It was as if the hand of God reached down and held back all those lanes of traffic. I re-started my Honda and steered off to the side of the road. The SUV stopped. Four college guys who said they were on their way to a basketball game, jumped out and asked me if I was okay. They said they thought for sure, I was dead. I must have been still in shock, because I exchanged information with the driver and was able to call a tow truck. As I looked down at his vanity plates, I read BEEFEE. My great-grandmother saved me from BEEFEE.

A Routine Mammogram

The third part of my career, fundraising, partially stemmed from a routine mammogram. One ordinary afternoon, my doctor's office called to say that it was time for my annual check-up. I went to see my doctor. She said everything was fine; just to be on the safe side, she wanted me to get a mammogram and an ultrasound.

I went to Women's College Hospital and sat in a room with 10 other women. Sitting there and waiting certainly makes you realize what is important in life. When the statistics are that 1 in 9 women get breast cancer now, that's pretty scary. I've had aunts, cousins and friends who have all had breast cancer. I vowed that whatever my results would be, I was going to do something for the cause. Besides, I owed something BIG to my guardian angel, Louissa.

I was finally dismissed from the waiting room. Unfortunately, I still had to wait another two weeks for my final results. The two-week wait made me even more determined to do something to help out in this fight against cancer. As it turned out, my results were fine. Who knows, those stats can change any day.

With the cooperation of Yuk Yuks, Standard Radio, and Princess Margaret Hospital, I co-created 'Laughlines' with Shari Cappe. **"Laughlines"** would be an evening of all-female stand-up comedy with proceeds being donated to breast cancer research. We worked every day on the project. As a result, the first of what would be six annual 'Laughlines' was a roaring success. We were packed to the rafters. In that six-year period, we raised over $650,000.

I have since taken the event to the Canadian Breast Cancer Foundation - to eventually launch a national campaign, **"Stand Up for the Girls"**. We had our first Toronto event this year at Yuk Yuks, with the support of Astral Radio, and it was also a great success. To see friends, family, and survivors in the audience was overwhelming. It was such an easy, fun event to do! To think, it all started out as a fundraising idea that only took fifteen minutes a day, still surprises me.

The Power of Generosity
Over my 15 year radio career, one of the most gratifying things I experienced was radio's tie-in to community, national and global charity events. Radio provided many of

these worthy causes with a voice. Of these causes, one of the most inspiring people I ever met was the CEO of World Vision - Dave Toycen. I was at the Mix at the time in Toronto and we were doing a Radiothon for World Vision. The idea was to encourage people to, for a small amount of money per month, adopt a child in a third world country. We interviewed Dave on the air. Afterwards, he gave me his book, "*The Power of Generosity*".

In his book, Dave said that the common denominator that determined whether or not a child was going to be generous to others was not gender based, or economically based or regionally based. The common denominator was this - if one or both parents were generous, then chances are, they would raise a child who was generous. That was mind blowing. Wow, what better gift to give the planet than the example of generosity?

The Influence of Our Parents

I was floored by this comment and it made me think back to my childhood. My father is generous with his skills. He will work on anybody's house or car and never takes a penny. My mother is generous with the less fortunate. She has a number of charities that she donates to. My parents aren't rich, but my mother, especially, is aware that there are people so much worse off than herself.

The generosity of my mother comes from the generosity of her mother and the generosity her grandmother, (Louissa).

Great-grandmother, Louissa left Barbados, by herself, in the 1800's, in her twenties, to find a better life in South America. She settled in Guyana. She cleaned houses and baked and sold products to the merchants that came into port. Whenever the day was over, Louissa would give any of her leftover goods that she didn't sell to the less fortunate around her. Louissa instilled this 'power of generosity' in her daughter - my Granny Cheong

My mother said that in the country, many times, someone would come to Granny Cheong's back door and say, "Mrs. Cheong. I don't have anything to eat. My family is hungry." Granny Cheong would never turn anybody away. She was not rich, but if she only had a half a cup of rice, she would give it to them.

My mother especially, is a generous person and I can see now how she became that way through her mother and her grandmother's examples. If I am generous, it's because of the great examples that my parents set. For that I am eternally grateful.

"The various physical, social and health activities of 2700 men were surveyed over the course of ten years. Those who did regular volunteer work had death rates two and a half times lower than those who did not." - The Power of Generosity

> *"We make a living by what we get, but we make a life by what we give."*
> *– Dave Toycen, The Power of Generosity*

Drive - The Surprising Truth about What Motivates Us

Another source of great inspiration for me was a book that I read by author Daniel H Pink titled, *"Drive -The Surprising Truth about What Motivates Us"*

Pink sites some of the top things that motivate us - one of them is altruism. Pink says, when human beings were first evolving, our basic needs were all extrinsic i.e.: food, water, warmth and sex. However he says, as our lives got easier, our needs became more INTRINSIC. In a nutshell, he says that human beings are now driven by three main intrinsic needs:

Autonomy - the need to create our own direction. (There are numerous studies showing successful Fortune 500 groups are sometimes more successful when they let their employees choose what they want to work on.)

Mastery - the need to improve ourselves (Mastery is one of the reasons why we pick up an instrument on weekends. None of us think we are going to be in the Rolling Stones, yet it feels great to get better at playing the piano or guitar.)

Altruism - the need to create something bigger than ourselves. (Pink says that altruism is really good for big business. People tend to want to work for, and stay with companies that give something back. Workers want to feel like they are part of a bigger picture - the common good.)

131

Educating the World For Free

The best example of big business altruism that Pink used was this; it was a classic case of David and Goliath. Pink cites the case of a very successful software company that paid staff to come up with an encyclopedia that would be sold on CD-ROMS and later on-line. In contrast, another company formed an encyclopedia based on information that experts and hobbyists donated to in the name of creating something that everyone could access for free. The results – Wikipedia, which contains more than 17 million donated articles, eventually forced Microsoft to abandon its MSN Encarta disc and on-line encyclopedia. Wikipedia was done in the name of educating the world for free.

Queen Oprah's 25 Year Farewell

Of course, one cannot talk about altruism and generosity without mentioning one of the most philanthropic celebrities that has graced our planet - Queen Oprah. Oprah has donated over $40 million for causes like education and programs for women and children. I'm still in grief-counselling since she took her show off of prime time.

I'll never forget her farewell episode. Even if you are not a fan of Oprah, you have to admit her message is powerful. You also have to admire her work ethic. In 25 years, 4561 shows, over 30,000 guests, in 150 countries, Oprah never missed a day!

Oprah started her last episode by saying that she always wanted to be a teacher. She WAS a teacher. We (her audience) were her classroom. In her last episode (sniff, sniff, I still get choked up thinking about it), Oprah left us with the following lessons:

1. **Be Yourself:** Start embracing the life that is calling you. You are responsible for your own life. Don't wait for someone else to save you or 'complete' you.
2. **Use your life to serve the world.**
3. **Ask yourself, what is YOUR platform?** What is and who is YOUR circle of influence?
4. **Don't confuse fame with service.** Not everyone has to be famous. Your influence could be one person or the people in your family who you influence every day.
5. **Energy:** "What is life? Life is energy. You are responsible for the energy that you bring to yourself and the energy that you bring to others."

Like Dave Toycen and author Daniel H Pink, Oprah exemplifies that it's all about giving back. The main part of Oprah's success didn't come from *seeking* wealth, but seeking to give a voice to those who didn't have one. Oprah's success came from helping and giving back; whether she was giving money or using her show to help others.

Do one thing for at least one other person, every day. It will change who you are.

***"From caring comes courage."* - Lao Tzu**

"People are like stained glass windows: They sparkle and shine when the sun is out, but when the darkness sets in, their true beauty is revealed only if there is light within. – Elizabeth Kubler-Ross

Chapter 12

Relieving Stress with Humour
- 7 Ingredients for Living Well That Don't Include Tofu!

"You're only given a little spark of madness - you mustn't lose it." - Robin Williams

Humour and passion can get you through many things. Laughing releases endorphins (natural pain killers) and serotonin (a neurotransmitter in the brain known as the 'happy hormone'). Laughing feels good. Some experts say that hard, belly laughter can actually have the same 'high' effect as heroin. In fact, there are studies now using humour to help recovering addicts. Humour is powerful. Look at political late night hosts like John Colbert, John Stewart or Bill Maher. Their political messages are sometimes very strong, yet accepted, because the delivery of the message is funny. Humour is the ultimate cure - the salve, the Band-Aid and/or the olive branch.

Passion is also a very powerful tool. Among other things, passion gives us focus. Passion makes us stick to something when others drop out. Through my comedy, radio, keynotes and fundraising, I've learned that humour and passion combined with the following seven ingredients are so powerful that they almost turn you into a Marvel Superhero. Be forewarned.

135

By the way, none of these ingredients involve eating tofu. Yay!!! (It's not the tofu that bothers me; it's the jelly they package it in. What is that??? blahhhh)

Okay, so put on your Marvel Superhero ring and check out 'The 7 Ingredients for Living Well that Don't Include Tofu'.

1. Positive Attitude
2. Perseverance
3. Forgiveness
4. Faith
5. Family
6. Friends
7. Activity - Physical and Mental

1. Positive Attitude
"A positive attitude may not solve all of your problems, but it will annoy enough people to make the effort worth it." Reader's Digest Hern Albright

I think my overall positive attitude and humour comes from both my parents. As kids, I remember my sisters and I weren't allowed to feel sorry for ourselves for too long. The threat, "Do you want me to give you something to cry about?" got a lot of mileage in our household. That's how my parents rolled. They were old school. They both came to Canada from humble beginnings. Humour and attitude played a big part in rolling with the punches. When something bad happened, we screamed, we cried, then, eventually, there was always a joke or a punch line.

Judy Croon

The Dalai Lama had a similar technique, but because he was the Dalai Lama, everyone thought that HE was hip and groovy. The Dalai Lama's book, *"The Art of Happiness"* remains one of my favourites. I love these two quotes in particular:

"Happiness can be achieved through training the mind."
and *"... personal happiness can manifest as a simple willingness to reach out to others, to create a feeling of affinity and goodwill, even in the briefest of encounters."*

Of course, the Dalai Lama is unique; there are also real life heroes walking amongst us every day. Take the story of a 90-year-old woman named Val Willis from Ottawa. Val lost her only daughter to cancer eight years earlier. I wondered how Val maintained her optimism after that catastrophic event. Val said, *"Most of us have experiences stored in memories that bless and burn. Can any tragedy be greater than the loss of a child or another beloved person, leaving us with consuming grief? Then - out of nowhere - comes a little voice reminding us it's time to count our blessings and rise above our despondency. Our grief is still part of us, but we realize we must move on, to do our share in making the world a happier place for others."* We should all remember Val Willis' story.

> *"Death leaves a heartache no one can heal,*
> *love leaves a memory no one can steal."*
> *~From a headstone in Ireland*

2. Perseverance

"When you come to the end of your rope, tie a knot and hang on." - Franklin D. Roosevelt

Oh there were times in comedy that I felt like I came to the end of my rope. Somehow, someway, I always managed to hold on. I think the knots came from a combination of passion, perseverance and not knowing any better - which sometimes is not such a bad thing!

"Don't worry about the world coming to an end today. It is already tomorrow in Australia. "Charles Schultz

3. Forgiveness

"To forgive is to set a prisoner free and discover that the prisoner was you." - Louis B Smedes

Go figure that one of my greatest life lessons came from a Clint Eastwood movie. It was the lesson of forgiveness. I was on a plane from Toronto to Halifax for a gig. No, Clint wasn't sitting beside me, but if he was I would have given him a big fat kiss. I was scrolling through the selection of in-flight movies. I stumbled upon one of Clint's flicks called "*Invictus.*" *Invictus* is the story about Nelson Mandela (played by Morgan Freeman) and South Africa's national rugby team. *Invictus* is the story of how Mr. Mandela, as the newly appointed Prime Minister of South Africa, used that country's rugby team as a symbol for unity during the 1961 World Rugby Championships. I never thought I'd care so much about rugby! At one point in the movie, Mr. Mandela gives the team's captain (Matt Damon) a poem called Invictus. Mr. Mandela says he read the poem to himself every day for 27 years while he was incarcerated on Robben Island. Mr. Mandela says it would have been easy for him to be angry at his captors on Robben Island. Instead, he chose to forgive them and learn from them.

INVICTUS (Imagine Morgan Freeman reading this!)

Out of the night that covers me,
Black as the Pit from pole to pole
I thank whatever gods may be
For my unconquerable soul.

In the fell clutch of circumstance
I have not winced nor cried aloud.
Under the bludgeonings of chance
My head is bloody, but unbowed.

Beyond this place of wrath and tears
Looms but the Horror of the shade,
And yet the menace of the years
Finds, and shall find, me unafraid.

It matters not how strait the gate,
How charged with punishments the scroll.
I am the master of my fate:
I am the captain of my soul.

- William Ernest Henley

Okay, picture me at this point, sitting on the plane in between two strangers crying. - AWKWARD. *Invictus* is a movie about victory; victory that comes only after there is forgiveness.

4. Faith

"Be faithful in small things because it is in them that your strength lies." - Mother Theresa

One day I was cooking dinner. Larry King was interviewing a gentleman by the name of Reverend Rick Warren. Warren is the founding pastor of Saddleback Church in Lake Forrest, California. It's one of the biggest churches in the United States. Warren is a pretty laid back guy. (I think he was wearing a Hawaiian shirt the night that he was speaking to Larry King). You might also remember Reverend Warren from President Barrack Obama's Inauguration Day in 2008. Warren gave the invocation prayer.

Here is one of my favourite quotes from that prayer.

1.

``We are so grateful to live in this land, a land of unequalled possibility, where the son of an African immigrant can rise to the highest level of our leadership. And we know today that Dr. King and a great cloud of witnesses are shouting in heaven."

- Reverend Warren

The day after the Larry King interview, I bought Warren's book, *"The Purpose Driven Life"* To this day, it remains in my top ten. The gist of the book is this:
(Note: Not everybody would agree with this and that's okay, but you're wrong...JUST kidding.)

God has a plan for each of us. *The Purpose Driven Life* is a 40-day personal journey to find the answer to the question, *"What on earth am I here for?"* If we were born for God's purpose, what is that purpose?

I'm still on my journey. However, I do believe that within my 15 minute a day obsessive compulsive way, I am slowly getting there.

By the way, if that white light at the end of a tunnel IS a 40 watt bulb, I'll be really mad.

5. Family
"Families are like fudge; mostly sweet, with a few nuts." – Anonymous

Every morning I count my blessings. One of those blessings is my immediate family, my extended family and then family friends. My sisters and I were very lucky. We never doubted for a moment that we were loved. Even now, my dad visits most weeks regularly to fix something in my house or my mom sends me home with leftovers. We have always been and remain a priority in our parent's lives. This is why it baffles me that they are not taking my calls. JUST kidding.

141

6. Friends

"My friends are my estate." - Emily Dickinson

I have friends and family all over the place. Again, I am blessed. My friends include people who I've known since grade school. A lot of those friends are also comics that I met and worked with over a weekend in some forgotten small town. It's amazing how fighting in the trenches at a comedy club, over a few days, will bond comics for life. No one else can understand what it's like when you 'kill' or 'destroy' or 'bomb'.

Finally, I can't mention the word friend, without mentioning my four-legged friend, Oskar. Oskar was a 130 pound Rottweiler who travelled with me sometimes - especially to the sketchier gigs in New York and New Jersey.

As big and scary as Oskar was, it amazed me how many customs officers, kids and total strangers reached into the car to pat him without asking if he was friendly or not. I guess the Canadian plates on the car gave away his friendliness. A Rottweiler from Canada would NEVER bite.

"Dogs are the leaders of the planet. If you see two life forms; one of them is making a poop, the other one's carrying it for him, who would you assume is in charge?" - Jerry Seinfeld

7. Activity
Physical Activity

"Me thinks the moment I begin to move, my thoughts begin to flow." - Henry David Thoreau

My final key to living well is activity - mental and physical. This is where my fifteen minute-a-day-slow-but–steady-pace really pays off.

I was one of those people who was athletic in high school, then afterwards HATED exercising. So, I chose to apply my fifteen minutes a day rule to the EASIEST form of physical activity I could think of – walking. Fifteen minutes a day turned into eventually forty-five minutes a day. Here's a good reason to consider walking.

Experts say that on average, you can extend your life by up to two minutes for every minute that you walk. Also every extra twenty minutes that you add to your walk a year, you burn seven pounds of body fat. (jorbins.com)

"I can only meditate when I'm walking. When I stop, my mind ceases to think; my mind only works with my legs." - Jean-Jacques Rousseau

Walking does the most important thing for me. It allows me to think. It allows me to create. Every day, I write and rehearse my material when I walk. Movement sparks creativity because exercise gets your neurons firing.

There is a Latin proverb that says, *"Solvitur ambulando"* (you can solve it by walking).

The Greek philosopher, Aristotle would walk around the *Lycium Gymnasium* in Athens and share his thoughts with his followers. Okay, not exactly the guy you want to have blabbing beside you on the Stepmaster, but it worked at the time. Did you know that those guys that followed Aristotle around at the gym became known as the Peripatetic school - which is derived from the Greek word *Pateo*, to walk! How cool is that?

Walking is not for wimps. Roman soldiers were expected to walk up to 40 Kms (25 miles) a day, carrying a 30 km backpack - in sandals! I'll never complain about my Nikes again.

Experts say that walking burns approximately the same amount of calories per mile as running does. Sure, it might take me twice as long and The Golden Girls could probably pass me, but what do I care?

Mental Activity
"There are worse crimes than burning books. One of them is not reading them." - Joseph Brodsky

Finally, what better way to stimulate our brains than reading? To be totally honest, stand-up comedy was not the first thing that I applied my fifteen minutes a day approach to. The real catalyst was reading. I was one of those people who would look at a book and say, "Heck, I'm never going to get through that." or "When will I have time to read seven hundred pages?" At some point in my life, I asked myself, "What if I just read fifteen minutes a day?"

What seemed like a stack of time, consuming books that I felt guilty not reading, eventually turned into bite-sized pages, chapters and novels that over time, entertained and enriched my life. Where would I be without books like: *"A Prayer for Owen Meany``, "A Fine Balance``, "The Razor's Edge``, "Jane Eyre``, "Wuthering Heights``, "Three Cups of Tea``, ``Life of Pi``, ``Eat Pray Love``, ``Emperor: The Gates of Rome`` (Conn Iggulden's brilliant "Julius Caesar" series),``The Help", ``The Purpose Driven Life``, ``The Motley Fool Investment Guide`` (this book should be called Investing for Dummies. It's brilliant. It saved me from the Dot Gone bust), ``The Shack``, ``The Secret Life of Bees``, ``The Life of Negroes", "Gods and Generals`` etc.*

Reading is one luxury that I've never EVER regretted. In fact, I regret not reading more.

"Man's mind stretched to a new idea never goes back to its original dimensions." - Oliver Wendell Holmes Jr.

Humor has had a huge impact on my life. The punch line to my life is that I would have never predicted what I would be doing in twenty years. That afternoon at the University of Calgary, I really thought my life was over when my dream of being a veterinarian was crushed.

As it turned out, my true passion lay in comedy. Comedy then led me to so many other unforeseen opportunities like radio, fundraising and keynote speaking. Comedy can be a *bit* egocentric (let's say you need big *'tah tahs'* to stand on stage) but with some humility, balance, and a 7 ingredient superhero ring, anything is a possible.

There is a saying, 'when a door closes, a window opens'. In my case, someone opened a window and 6 generations of fruit flies and 75% of my final mark escaped. It was the best thing that could have happened to me. As I look back on it now; I would have been too soft to be a veterinarian. Ironically, I'm like Teflon when I stand on stage.

A Japanese proverb says, 'fall seven times; stand up eight.'

In my case I chose 'stand-up' comedy. The adventures (the good, the bad and the ugly) were endless. I'll never regret any of them.

Where to from here? My primary goal is to take *'Stand Up For the Girls'* national. After that, I'll continue doing what I'm doing until I'm 90 years old - fifteen minutes at time.

PART IV

By Susan Stewart

About the Author / Introduction

After leaving stand-up comedy, Susan then found herself working in a Human Resources branch within the Ontario Government. Comedy to Human Resources... a natural progression, don't you think? Ahem. Throughout her shockingly enjoyable and passionate career as an organizational learning and development consultant, Susan became inspired to get back on stage and use her comedic powers for good, rather than evil!

Since 2005, Susan has been traveling around Canada helping people see the lighter side of work and life. With her memorable high energy and quick wit, Susan has rocked the mic for many private and public-sector organizations, school boards, universities, and associations.

Susan is a contributing author of three other self-development books: *Awakening the Workplace-Volume 3; The Master Mind Group;* and *Bushido Business.*

Along with sharing lessons that she has learned from her own experiences, Susan's chapters explore how spirituality and living with a higher awareness of your perceptions and thoughts can help you lighten up about the inevitable changes and challenges that come our way in this thing called life.

To learn more about Susan, visit <u>www.susanstewart.ca</u>

Chapter 13

From Stand-Up Comedy to Human Resources: What the Heck Happened & the Lessons I Learned

Before I got involved in writing and professional speaking, I did stand-up comedy for about five years. In those five years, I performed at various comedy clubs in Toronto and around Ontario. During my five years in comedy, I also toured across Canada for three summers with three different one-woman shows. That was my time in comedy and I'm proud to say that I experienced a little success...as much success as one can experience doing stand-up comedy for five years in Canada – a few free meals and a sweet discount on the domestic beers at the bar. After five years of trying to be the next big thing in Canadian stand-up comedy, I quit. The reason I quit stand-up comedy is that I took myself and my work far too seriously. Before I go any further with the story, feel free to take a moment to choke on the irony of the last statement. Yes, I was a comedienne who struggled like hell to lighten up about life. Ahem. Even though I loved the art of standing on stage and making people laugh, I had this collection of negative and fearful thoughts that would play over and over again in my head. Nobody else had to criticize me because I was doing a fine job of it myself. Have you ever had that

149

moment, when you realize that the one person you're the most tired of being around, is you? I was basically walking around with this tape of negative thoughts playing on a loop and the messages were like the antithesis of a self-help audio book. The tape I was listening to was more like a volume of greatest hits of put-downs based on the belief that I wasn't good enough. The thoughts in my head were all a bunch of crap, but when you listen to those negative thoughts and worse yet, believe them, those false statements can appear very real. Oprah once said, "*You are not your thoughts.*" I think Oprah's on to something because being a comedienne and a heckler at the same time just doesn't make any sense.

> **Have you ever had that moment, when you realize the person you're most tired of being around, is you?**

Eventually, my mind-chatter caused me so much pain that I decided to leave stand-up comedy. I thought leaving stand-up comedy would give me a shot at feeling better, because at that point, I didn't understand the significant role my thoughts were playing in my unhappy experience. I thought that if my external circumstances and surroundings were different, I would be happy.

After I left stand-up, I had no idea what I was going to do next – I had no back-up plan whatsoever. Thankfully in this lifetime, when one door shuts (whether we close that door ourselves or it's slammed in our face) another door inevitably opens. Thankfully endings are very much beginnings. Thankfully I wasn't playing in the traffic very long. Shortly after leaving stand-up comedy, I landed a job in a Human Resources department in the Ontario Government. Yes, stand-up comedy to Human Resources or as I like to think of it, *stand-up comedy to sit-down comedy*. As I was sitting there at my desk, in my cubicle in the Ontario Government, I was rather tempted to get back into stand-up comedy because man, I had so much new material!

Even though I had dramatically changed up my external circumstances and surroundings, my mind-chatter continued. With my situation being very different from before, the tape in my head was playing a slightly different collection of negative and fearful thoughts; the effects were all very familiar. Even though I made about the most severe career change possible, I was in the same miserable place. My experience hadn't changed because my thoughts hadn't changed. In one of his books about mindfulness, Jon Kabat-Zinn, perfectly summarizes my findings during my pursuit of happiness when he says, "*where ever you go, there you are.*"

Have an "Attitude of Gratitude"
"*The hardest arithmetic to master is that which enables us to count our blessings.*" – Eric Hoffer

151

Looking back on the early days of my Human Resources career, I wish I had lowered the volume on my mind-chatter by taking on what my yoga teacher calls, "an attitude of gratitude". One thing I have learned over the last few years is that stress and gratitude simply cannot exist at the same time. Especially when a change or a challenge enters our lives, we have this opportunity to lighten up by realizing how good we truly have it; how much we do have; and how many things are going well! For example, people get all stressed out in traffic-jams as they sit in their cars – their cars! Those things are expensive and hey, I'm pretty sure that no matter how bad the traffic, walking would take much longer. Instead of huffing and puffing and honking our horns as we sit on the highway, we can take a look at how lucky we are to be driving in the first place and say, "Wow! Look at me in my car!" At the grocery store, some people stand in the checkout lines looking completely disgusted with life. The expression on their faces is a combination of frustration and looking like they're working through a severe gas pain. These people are fortunate enough to be in a store that has all kinds of food available in one place and they're waiting to buy this food with all of their money! Rather than rolling their eyes and sighing out loud as they flip through the latest issue of *People Magazine*, they could stand there and say, "Wow! Look at me in a grocery store!" In this age of abundance where we have vast amount of access to and choice of goods and

Susan Stewart

services, I do believe our expectations have become rather warped. We could use a little reality check to help us notice and appreciate how blessed we are.

If you are up for a little more irony, our modern conveniences have led to the creation of more stressful thoughts than less. You'll see the irony I'm referring to if you do an online search for the "happiest places on earth". These places don't have nearly the amount of material and economical abundance that we do, but the people report a much higher rate of contentment than those living the supposed "better life" in North America. Bless us and our first world problems. Have you noticed the horror on people's faces when their cell phone signal drops mid-conversation and they have to call someone back? In our hands, we are holding phones that used to be attached to our kitchen wall! Didn't we love the kitchen phone with its mile-long cord that made it possible to chat with someone while we folded the laundry, made our bed, and reorganized the garage? Now we can roam the entire earth with the kitchen phone and we complain about roaming charges! Not only are we holding the kitchen phone in our hands, but now most of us are holding a computer as well! Ah, but we'll be damned if our phone is slow connecting us on to the Internet! These phones of ours basically send and receive magical signals to and from mars and if takes a few seconds longer to do that, we call it a piece of crap and we want a new one. Rather than curse and growl in that moment, we could simply smile as Facebook uploads on to the screen, and say, "Wow! Someone I hardly know wants to be my friend!" So, anytime you're sitting in traffic, roll down your window, smile at the guy in the lane beside you, and yell, "WOW! Look at us in our cars!" Now, you're probably going to get the finger, but you'll be feeling so good it won't matter.

If only I knew then, what I know now. I mean, hey, there were some serious perks to having my new "real job". For example, I got to wake-up in the morning and leave my house (a comedienne in the morning usually returns to their house), every two weeks someone put money into my bank account (you don't get *that* in comedy), and hey, I had free access to the Internet all day long! If only I had noticed how blessed I truly was, it would have been impossible to create stressful thoughts at the same time.

Change Your Thoughts, Change Your Experience
"When you change the way you look at things, the things you look at change." – Wayne Dyer

One particular stressful thought that played over and over in my head was that this change from stand-up comedy to Human Resources was never going to be anything but a random act of a comedienne who was washed up by the age of 28. Even though I held a life-long belief that everything and everyone that enters our life is well-planned, orchestrated, and purposeful, I sat there under the sharp glow of the office fluorescents thinking that maybe, just maybe, this was the one time the universe just simply screwed up. When things in your personal or professional life have taken an unexpected turn, have you ever had the feeling that even the universe is completely shocked and thoroughly confused by what has happened? I envisioned one of my angels casually floating by above me, noticing me sitting at my desk and saying, "Holy crap! Who put the comedienne in the cubicle?!?!" That angel then would wave another one of my angels over to show them the awkward scene below. Pointing right at me, the other angel would then say, "Look, the poor thing doesn't even know how to cut and paste! Remember the right-click, baby! It's all there for you! Oh look, now she's crying." Both angels would be staring down at the shocking turn of events not knowing how this could have happened. For about a year, I had the feeling there was no rhyme or reason to this major change in my life. The anxiety I was dealing with on a daily basis got to be too much to handle, I decided it was time to do something about it. Still rather unaware of the role my thoughts were playing in my unhappy experience, I decided to quit.

Being a newbie in the "real world", I didn't know how someone went about quitting a "real job". I also didn't bother finding out. I simply stood up from my desk, walked over to my boss' office and told her, "I quit". My boss,

Nancy, knew the kind of girl she was dealing with and all she did was smile and ask me to go home that night and think about it. Nancy said, *"If you still want to leave tomorrow, I will officially accept your resignation."* What a drama queen. I agreed to think about it and confirm my decision the next day. As I sat at home that evening, it occurred to me that once again, I didn't have a back-up plan and that there was a possibility that the job fairy was on a sabbatical and wouldn't be available to land another opportunity in my lap like she did so beautifully the last time. I wish I had some Oprah "a-ha moment" that night, that I could insert at this point in the chapter; truth be told, because I had no idea what to do next, I decided to stay. It may have felt like fear and a wavering faith in the universe, but what I was really doing by deciding to stay was more an act of surrendering and allowing life to unfold. That night, a powerful shift took place within me that led me to the lightness that we can feel when we let go and live in the mystery.

The next day at work, I stuck my head into Nancy's office, flashed a sheepish grin and said, "Just kidding." My decision to stay and forge ahead in my new Human Resources career wasn't without its moments of self-awareness. I realized that if I was going to remain in the job I wanted to enjoy it more and that being happier just might be an inside job. I decided that it was up to me to view this change differently so the experience was well, different. I made a few changes to how I viewed this new chapter in my life. Firstly, I stopped arguing with reality and accepted where I was in my journey. I also detached from my past, stopped trying to figure out the future, and wrapped my arms around the present. Beyond deciding to plant both of my feet in the present, I also realized that it was time to chill out. I showed up to work each day with the intention to lighten up, have more fun, and rock out HR! I know rocking out HR seems like a bit of a stretch; what I am getting at is that I began to see my life and my career change as the adventure it truly was. When I finally changed to better thoughts the experience changed for the better.

Change Doesn't Happen *To* You, Change Happens *For* You

A few months after I decided to stay put in my HR career, a colleague of mine named Janice came to me with a proposition. Janice was on a committee of people who were organizing a professional development conference for one of the ministries our Human Resources branch supported and the theme of the conference was wellness. Janice and the rest of the committee wanted me to put together a comical presentation about all the major aspects of healthy living. What this committee didn't understand was that I was still pretty fresh out of stand-up comedy... I was still drinking and smoking quite heavily. I hadn't exercised in about twelve years. I was just a solid example

157

of what not to do. After Janice presented the opportunity to me, my knee-jerk reaction was to turn it down flat, instead I actually slowed everything down, took a step back, and really thought about it. I then I had a huge epiphany. I thought to myself, "Hey, this means a day out of the office!" With the thought of being able to crawl out from my cubicle and get back on stage, I told Janice that I would do it on the condition that she would do it with me and be my straight-man. Hey, you can take the girl out of comedy, but...

After several weeks of intense research and a little personal change, Janice and I got up in front of the crowd of public sector employees wearing matching sweat bands and wielding heads of broccoli as we debuted the rollicking good time also known as, *"LIVE WELL, LAUGH LOTS"*. Janice and I had a blast and everyone really liked it! We started to get phone calls and emails from people requesting us to come to their event and deliver our smash-hit presentation. I was ecstatic and Janice was mortified. Despite Janice's mixed feelings about our fast rise to stardom, we were in demand and we were taking the show on the road! We were busy delivering our smash-hit presentation at all kinds of Ontario government events and meetings. When I told my mother what was going on she said, *"Susan, leave it to you to go get a government job, and still manage to go out on tour!"*

Eventually Janice stepped away from the tour and with her blessing; I continued doing the presentation on my own which grew into other wellness-based workshops and speeches. For a couple of years, I was busy with both my Human Resources career and my budding speaking business. I worked long days at the government and then took time off to speak at events. One day Janice (who had become my boss) called me into her office and told me that my double-life wasn't working out anymore. Janice told me that it was time to choose between HR and my speaking career. I decided to take the leap of faith. Well, first I cried and called my mother and then I took the leap of faith. I've been combining my stand-up comedy skills with inspirational messages ever since. The name of my business is appropriately and sentimentally called, **LIVE WELL, LAUGH LOTS.**

It turns out those angels knew what they were doing the whole time. It may not be pretty at the time, but eventually, we see how a change in our personal or professional life served us in some way. Down the road we see how a change taught us a lesson, brought us an insight, delivered us a message, taught us a skill, or provided us with a chance to grow. The trick is to have the faith that the magic never goes away. When we resist or are fearful of change, it's because we convince ourselves that all that magic in the past couldn't possibly be at work right now. Look for the magic by remembering all the evidence from your past that proves that change ends up being a gift. When we are mindful of the past data we have about change, we can enter a state of curiosity about how this new change will end up serving us in some way. You most likely have at least one situation from your past that proves that change is a gift. If you can't think of anything from your past right now, don't worry, it will come to you. For now, just remember my story because if a girl can go from stand-up comedy to a job in a Human Resources department in the Ontario government and it all made perfect sense in the end, there's hope for us all!

> **It turns out those angels knew what they were doing the whole time.**

Chapter 14
MY FRIEND, MR. DEPRESSION

Despite doing stand-up comedy for five years and now being an inspirational speaker, seeing the lighter side of life actually doesn't come naturally to me. For me to be peaceful, positive, and generally light-hearted throughout changes and challenges requires living with a high level of awareness. By awareness, I mean consciously choosing to view and think about things in ways that work for me rather than against me. Honestly, if I'm not careful, I can easily become a depressed and anxious inspirational speaker. God, I wish I was kidding with you right now, but Mr. Depression and I go way back. We met back in 2002 and it's been a love-hate relationship ever since. The love exists due to the fact that my experiences with depression transformed me into the more "awakened" person I am today. Because stressful thoughts trigger the release of hormones such as cortisol that bring on symptoms of depression, I have become very inspired to be more aware of the thoughts I create. Well, that and my rather straight-shooting mother saying to me, *"You know Susan, every time you get like this, you're shortening your life."* I would then smile at her and thank her very much for the pick-me-up. Those conversations with my mother also gave me the desire to live a more conscious life. I wanted to see things differently because 99% of all illnesses are connected to stressful thoughts.

You might be wondering why I keep on saying "stressful thoughts", rather than "stress". One of the pieces of awareness I received from hanging out with Mr. Depression is that there really is no such thing as stress – not in the way that people commonly view it and refer to it in conversation. If you have noticed, many people refer to stress as this condition that is very separate from them. I often hear people talk about avoiding stress and finding peace, but because the stress response and relaxation response kicks in depending on the thoughts we create and

> **Avoid being stressful, and find ways to be peaceful.**

feelings we have, I have no reason not to believe that what really is at hand for us is to avoid *being stressful,* and find ways to *be peaceful.* We tend to talk about stress like it's something that just swoops in the room or we can carry it our purse. Stress is commonly viewed as this invisible swamp-thing that just body-slams you when you're not looking and all of a sudden you're a complete wreck. I typically hear people say something like, *"There's just so much stress at work right now."* For me, that conjures up an image of that person's workplace covered in stress - stress hanging from the ceiling, draped over everyone's desk, and stuffed into the filing cabinets. Clear expression

Susan Stewart

of separation - I stand here and stress is over there at work and there's so much of it. *"We've got that meeting tomorrow – that's going to bring on a lot of stress."* From that statement, I picture someone sending *stress* a meeting request through Microsoft Outlook and it showing up, sitting around the boardroom table, and injecting everyone with a good dose of anxiety. A very popular phrase nowadays is, *"I'm under a lot of stress."* From that I visualize someone's boss walking out of their office pushing a gigantic boulder of fear, frustration, and anger towards that person and completely flattening them with it. I rarely hear anyone take accountability for being stressed. There is no situation I can recall where someone has said, *"We've got that meeting tomorrow – that's going to lead me to creating a lot of stressful thoughts."* The fact of the matter is that the stress response (short-lived or chronic) cannot exist without first creating stressful thoughts. Mr. Depression taught me that stronger mental health is truly a few new thoughts away.

Depression turned out to be a powerful gift in my life because without fun times such as not wanting to get out of bed in the morning, withdrawing from my friends and family, and losing my appetite (*okay, that one sort of came in handy*), I'm not sure if I ever would have been so determined to challenge my stressful thoughts. Depression showed me the power of the mind-body connection and how to use it for good, rather than evil. I'm now very

163

inspired to lighten up about the stuff that used to drag me down, because the brain translates every emotion into a chemical equivalent. In the biggest nutshell ever, positive feelings trigger the release of health-enhancing endorphins and calming neurotransmitters. Negative feelings trigger the release of a large amount of destructive stress hormones in our system – when hormones such as cortisol and norepinephrine are at high levels in our system, the level of those good feeling chemicals are dragged down and we can feel some degree of the "blues" and/or anxiety.

Since I've endured the downside of the mind-body connection (stress hormones high, endorphins low), I figure I might as well share what I've learned from the experience. What Mr. Depression taught me was that despite its miraculous design, the body has a major flaw in its system. The bodily dysfunction I am referring to is that the body can't tell the difference between *real* danger and *perceived* danger. Our body releases stress hormones when we're running out of a burning building and it releases those same stress hormones when we're running around worrying about the latest drama at work. The body can't decipher whether our fearful feelings are truly justified and it doesn't have the ability to save stress hormones for times when only real danger is at hand. Nope, our thoughts about work and our personal lives are triggering a stress response in our body that was created to help us survive in danger, when let's admit it, most of the time, we are so *not*

Susan Stewart

in danger. With all the stressful thoughts we tend to crank out and all the fear we feel, our bodies must think we're pretty damn brave to be venturing out into the world each day!

Once I realized that Mr. Depression and I were good buddies, because my body was responding to all the perceived danger I was fearful of, I began the journey of trying to be more mindful of my thoughts. I became a passionate seeker to find ways of being, that could help me tell my body that in spite of the challenges I was facing, I was most definitely safe. I want to share with you some mindfulness strategies that can keep those stress hormone levels good and low...

Focus On the Truth Rather Than the Story
***"The primary cause of unhappiness is never the situation but your thoughts about it."* - Eckhart Tolle**

One of the most profound realizations I've had in my life, so far (aside from the day I turned 30 and accepted the fact that I was not going to dodge the aging process as planned) is that all events, situations, and people who enter our lives, are neutral. Contrary to popular opinion, nothing comes to us as anything more than what it factually is. Even though we hear people say, "This is such a stressful week", the truth is that it's just a week containing certain appointments, meetings, tasks, etc. No week

165

comes with a tag attached to it saying, "I'm stressful – start freaking out now." Even though we hear people say, "*I work with some stressful people*", no one actually walks up to someone at work with a tag hanging from their arm that says, "*I am here merely to piss you off.*" Now, right now, you might think I'm some crazy person who doesn't have a firm grip on reality, but it's by drawing our attention to the observed reality rather than our imagined reality that can help us lighten up. We describe rainy days as "crappy"; the only thing that is real or true is that precipitation is falling from the sky... it's wet outside. Seeing things and people as stressful or rainy days as crappy, are the interpretations and meanings we place on neutral things and people. Yes, there are challenging weeks and challenging people, however, for anything or anyone to be stressful, we must see it that way.

Society has deemed certain neutral things as stressful for so long that we now have a tough time thinking of them in a different way. The master list of "stressful things" includes: weddings, divorces, starting new jobs, moving, and the holidays - and God bless us that we even view time off to celebrate a season with friends and family as a total pain in the ass. All those things on that previously mentioned list and all the other "stressful" things in life may very well be challenges; anything above and beyond that exists from the layer of "dramatic goop" we smack down on top of the cold, hard facts. Our perception of things and

Susan Stewart

people can easily shift our focus away from the truth and move it towards something bigger and often many times scarier. We create a story, based on the interpretation and meaning we place on stuff, as the facts of a situation or event goes through our personal filter; more technically referred to as *our perception.*

Perhaps you've placed a pile of "dramatic goop" on to a change or challenge and made it into something bigger and scarier. Maybe you've driven home from work thinking about something that happened during the day and as you were replaying the situation over in your mind you ended up looking like one of those soap opera characters having a flashback, remembering the time you were kidnapped and held captive in a cave for several months. After all the interpretation and meaning you placed on that certain change or challenge, you arrived home and your wife/husband/partner asked you how your day was and you exclaimed, "Sit down! You gotta hear this!" You then launched into a one-person show so they could fully appreciate what you had just been through. The stories in our minds often lead us to looking and sounding more like soldiers returning home from war rather than people returning home from work.

There is a powerful opportunity to decrease the amount of times we're telling our bodies we're in danger (and hence, lower the levels of stress hormones) by challenging the stories in our minds and focusing more on the truth. Yes, perhaps there are changes occurring or challenges that you are facing, but what else are you saying that is making it out to be much bigger and scarier than it actually is?

Watch Your Words

"Mastery is not measured by the number of terrible things you eliminate from your life, but by the number of times you eliminate calling them terrible." – Neale Donald Walsch

During a session with my therapist, I used the word "crisis" to describe what I was then going through. My therapist stopped me mid-sentence and said, *"Susan, watch your words."* She continued on and said, *"What's a crisis?"* I sat there with a blank look on my face knowing that this was some sort of trick question. I guess she knew my reply was going to be a bit of a wait because she answered for me. *"A crisis is when someone's life is in danger. If you have to pick up the phone and call 9-1-1, that's a crisis. Anything else and you're facing a challenge."* In that moment, I realized that the dramatic words we choose to describe changes or challenges are tiny stories that can cause us to feel things that indicate to our bodies that we're in danger. With this powerful lesson in awareness, I became concerned for the whole of society because if you listen to people talk, words such as, "crisis",

Susan Stewart

"disaster", and "tragedy" are used to describe almost every bloody challenging thing that comes our way.

Now that I try to watch my words when talking about things, I have become hyper-aware of when people don't watch their words. I was at an LCBO store (Liquor Control Board Of Ontario) located in mid-town Toronto and on that day there was a fancy shmancy wine sale happening in about a half-hour's time. The red wine that they were selling was so fancy that it was $150 per bottle. You can imagine my disappointment when I learned that they were limiting each purchase to one bottle per customer. Drat. When the wine sale was mere minutes away, I noticed two LCBO employees leaning up against a wall looking rather in pain about the whole impending situation. As I walked by them I overheard the female employee ask her male counter-part, "*Which one of us is going to be handling this fiasco?*" In my hyper-awareness, the use of the word, "fiasco", didn't slip by me. A *fiasco?* A *wine fiasco*? When the LCBO threatens to go on strike, that could result in a fiasco (heck, maybe even a crisis), but this wine sale was nothing more than a challenge.

Catch yourself in the act when you use dramatic words to describe a challenge. Avoid using words like "bombshell" to describe a change you just heard about and reserve it for when you see an attractive blonde woman like me walk by. It's a little thing. However, watching your words can be a powerful act of awareness that can help you manage that major flaw in the body's system.

Put Your Crystal Ball Away
"A thought is harmless unless we believe it. It's not our thoughts, but the attachment to our thoughts that causes suffering." – Byron Katie

Another way I have learned to keep those stress hormone levels low is by noticing and challenging my predictions about the future. I don't know about you, but I can be one hell of a busy fortune-teller. Whenever you speak of the future with any amount of certainty, you can bet that's a form of a story, because you're talking about something that hasn't happened yet. Unlike professional fortune-tellers, who only tell you good stuff, our amateur predictions typically forecast negative outcomes. *"This week is going to be insane."* or *"This meeting is going to be a total waste of my time."* or *"She's going to freak right out when she hears this!"* If we're going to bother lugging around crystal balls we might as well be sharing positive news.

Beyond telling frightful stories about what's to come, when we tell ourselves or other people how it's going to be, that's also limiting thinking. Predicting the future is like looking out at the countless possibilities of the future and narrowing those possibilities down to one option and throwing it in a zip lock bag for later. Can you see how you've placed limits on the future through telling yourself or the people around you how it's going to be? I'll share an example from my own life. I was jogging toward the lakeshore in Toronto and beyond me in the distance was a group of teenage boys. When I realized that I was going to have to jog around them and then in front of them wearing my tight-fitting workout clothes, I started predicting their reaction when my rear-end was going to be front and centre for them. As I jogged along, I started preparing myself for the derogatory remarks, the sexist comments, and the cat-calls (if I was lucky!). As I jogged closer to the group carrying my crystal ball (so it was quite a workout), I was anticipating and dreading what was about to happen. The monumental moment finally arrived. As I approached the group, I jogged around them and then jogged in front of them leaving them with a clear view of my tightly clad rear-end. At first there was silence and then all of a sudden, one of the boys from the group yelled out, "*I believe in you!*" A few moments later, the whole group of boys cheered. That was it! The experience of jogging around and in front of those boys wasn't only positive, it was rather uplifting.

How many times do you predict and put limits on the future like I did with that group of teenage boys? How many times does your body think it's in danger because you're convinced something negative is going to happen like I assumed those giant walking hormones were going to misbehave? By living more consciously, see if you can challenge your clairvoyant ways and remind yourself that because you don't know what's going to happen in the future, everything is possible!

Be Here Now

The stressful thoughts that cause those negative feelings that trigger the body to release stress hormones are all due to the "dramatic goop" we place on the past and/or the future. With that in mind, another effective way to keep stressful thoughts at a minimum is to focus on the present moment. It's very powerful and very challenging to live in the "now". I will often be driving home thinking about all kinds of things connected to the past or the future – not one of my thoughts will pertain to the fact that I'm operating a heavy piece of machinery that's in motion. I'll pull into my driveway, park my car, sit back and think to myself, "*Now, how the hell did I get here?*" I think we humans easily drift away from where we are and get wrapped up in one of our stories about the past or the future. When you're in the shower in the morning, check and see if you're in the shower. How many times are you already at that meeting or having that conversation with your boss? How many times have you showered with the people you work with? I can always tell when I'm not present in the shower because I'll stop thinking for a moment and realize that I have no idea if I've put the conditioner in my hair yet. I even find it challenging to be in the present moment when

I'm away on vacation. Even though I'm relaxing on the beach or shopping in a big, cosmopolitan city, I'll easily start replaying something that happened in the past or start predicting the future. Maybe I'll start sending postcards with a note that says, *"Having a great time! Wish I was here!"*

The quieter mind we have when we bring our full attention to the present moment, is precisely why meditation is a practice that can help someone transition out of depression and anxiety. I find traditional deep breath meditation agonizing and boring. If I need to sit down and write a to-do list, I go and meditate because that list will be done in seconds. I've tried meditation CDs – those things are great, because while I'm listening to it, I unload the dishwasher, pay my bills online, and tidy my office. As you can tell, being quiet isn't really my thing, so thank goodness for play. Fun is basically a casual form of meditation. When I'm out golfing or curling, my mind is completely focused on the game and I'll be given the gift of a quiet mind for a few hours. The meditative quality to play is why involving ourselves in our joys and passions has been found to lower blood pressure, boost the immune system, and yes, lower stress hormones. That is why the best time to play (even for a half hour) is when you don't have time to play.

It's simply not realistic to think that you're never going to crank out another story as long as you live, and that you'll only live in the present moment; it is realistic to make a pact with yourself that you intend on catching yourself in the act and making a shift back to the truth and back to the "now". Depression was indeed a gift – because of those days in the darkness, I am now a passionate seeker to find ways to manage the body's flaw in the system. It's because of depression that I live with a higher awareness of my thoughts and choose to see the lighter side of life.

Susan Stewart

Chapter 15

Your New Lenses Are Ready For Pick-Up: Seeing the Lighter Side of Life

"The true journey of discovery consists not in seeking new landscapes but in having fresh eyes." - Marcel Proust

I was having coffee with a friend, when she asked me what I talk about, when I deliver a speech or a workshop. I gave her a summary of my key messages and then said, *"Basically, I help people see the lighter side of life."* My friend smiled and told me that she yearned for the ability to laugh things off. As I shared the same yearning, I told her that I believe seeing the lighter side of life has very little to do with having a sense of humour. She stared back at me with a perplexed look on her face (the same one she gave me when I told her I wasn't interested in watching *Dancing with the Stars*) and then asked me to explain what I was talking about. I told her that my version of seeing the lighter side of life is seizing the opportunity to view the events, situations, and people in our lives from a higher perspective. I suggested to her that the perception we have of life is similar to wearing a particular set of lenses. We observe things, and then, depending on the perception we have (the lenses we are viewing things through) our experience is formed. I told her to think of her perception

175

(her set of lenses) as the moment when she interprets and attaches meaning to something or someone. I said to her, **"I think seeing the lighter side of life is wearing a set of lenses that helps you see things in a way that creates less drama and helps someone be peaceful no matter what changes or challenges come their way."** The higher perspective that we can have is much like being able to adjust the "zoom" setting when you're on the Internet looking at an image on Google Maps or Google Earth. When you zoom out and increase the scope of the view, it helps you see the "bigger picture". This higher perspective of events and situations allows us to see the grand design, how everything seems to fit together; the perfection of it all. When we see things at "ground level", we're left with a very limited view that suggests that there is nothing more going on than what we see right in front of us and the (often dramatic, stress-response-inducing) interpretation and meaning we place on it.

You might be sitting there right now, much like my friend at the coffee shop, enjoying listening to what I have to say, but at the same time wondering what the hell I'm really getting at. You might be reading this chapter wondering how these lenses, or a higher perspective, can really help someone be peaceful no matter what comes their way. I don't know if these lenses can end all suffering, but yes, they can significantly reduce the amount of times when a gin and tonic really seems like the best choice of breakfast

Susan Stewart

beverage. This higher perspective we can have is based on the belief that we are spiritual beings having a human experience. Our souls are down here on earth wearing these "human suits" and enduring things like menstrual cramps, baby showers, and heartache, all in the name of learning lessons through experiences. You are having your particular human experience to do just that - to experience certain things that will edge you further along in your evolution. When we "zoom out" and see things from that higher perspective, we see how our souls are perfectly placed in specific situations with specific people to learn and grow. Meanwhile at ground level, it appears like another argument with your teenager, another conflict with someone at work, or another messy break-up.

Wearing these lenses has helped me lighten up when I could so easily be wandering around in the dark. Your new lenses are ready for pick-up and here's how they improve your vision...

Things Don't Suck Just For The Sake Of Sucking
"The world is the great gymnasium where we come to make ourselves strong." - Swami Vivekananda, Indian Philosopher and Spiritual Leader

With the perspective that we are a bunch of souls or spirits hanging out down here on earth, in human form to experience different things, so we can learn, grow, and evolve, then nothing that typically is seen as bad, stressful or annoying can be merely taken at face value. When you really think about it, if our souls left the comforts of another dimension, where there are no such things as calories, traffic-jams, or winter weather, just so it could have a crack at the human experience, then what I know for sure is that no matter what comes our way in life, *things don't suck just for the sake of sucking.*

Early on in my speaking career, I was hired to deliver a lunchtime keynote speech at a conference that was to have roughly five hundred people in the audience. I was delighted to receive the opportunity to speak to such a large crowd and was excitedly anticipating the sound of that many people laughing all at once. I arrived at the event and found out that I was going to be speaking while the audience was in the buffet line and eating their lunch. Five hundred people in the audience and not one person heard a word I said. Everyone was too busy talking and eating lasagna, to notice the blonde woman bouncing up and down on the stage. When I finished my talk, I walked briskly out of the venue trying to look like I had somewhere really important to get to. Once safely in the confines of my car I cried. I cried for a few minutes (emotions come with our "human suit") and then I felt quite peaceful because I could see the perfection of it all. I could see that I was placed in that situation to have that experience. That experience was a grooming of sorts – it taught me to only accept speaking engagements that had me scheduled to speak before lunch or after lunch *because the lasagna always wins.*

People Are Being Difficult On Purpose

"When I'm having trouble with someone, it's a sure sign that person is exactly the gift I am needing in my life. Sometimes it takes me years to write the thank you note, though." – unknown

The challenging relationships we have (and those we lose) just might be one of life's greatest sources of suffering. One of the most powerful things we can do to be peaceful is to see that people are sent to us as teachers so we can grow in some way and learn certain lessons. The relationships we have with our colleagues, friends, family members, and romantic partners come into our lives with the number one mission to rock our world in some way. If you look back and see all that you have gained from your past professional and personal relationships, it's pretty clear to see how we humans are like chess pieces being moved and placed in close proximity with other souls who are to shape our life in some way. As I look back on my life, I can clearly see that the people in both my professional and personal lives, who brought about anger, pain, tears, and more phone calls to my mother than I would like to admit, were just doing their jobs – they stopped me in my tracks, they widened my eyes, they

179

showed me stuff I needed to see - they were all messengers delivering some kind of wake-up call. Did it suck? Big time. Did it hurt? Hell, yeah. Did it rock my world just when it needed rocking in a certain way? Absolutely. I should send each of them a rather lengthy thank you note.

We're All Bozos on the Bus

Like many people, I was once married. We were so happy that we decided to defy the odds and tie the knot. Three and a half years later, we were separated. In an attempt to make me feel better, my mother said, "*It's okay dear. Everyone should get married at least once.*" After we separated, I went through a long period of astonishment that we didn't make it and self-blame for the part I played in it all. In my darkest days after the separation, I was reading a spiritual book to help me cope with the loss and I read a quote by Wavy Gravy who is a clown/activist. Wavy says, "*We're all bozos on the bus so we might as well sit back and enjoy the ride.*" After I read that quote, I felt some of the shame and blame lift from my heart. I was reminded that we all are doing our very best based on what we know and what we've experienced so far. We were always going to say and do the things we did during the relationship, because that was the point we were both at in our journeys – we both did our very best. Wavy Gravy's quote lifted my spirit and reminded me that we're all bumbling around growing from human experiences such as relationships. With this awareness, one could go as far to say that

Susan Stewart

n in our professional and personal lives
it isn't.

romantic relationships has been a
c   out my adult life. Have you ever
r   e same lessons over and over
a   your ways? You trip up and
                     ntil you eventually get the
                     persistent that way. First it
                     you on the shoulder, and
                     over the head with its
                     e, I officially received
                     , I learned well, and I
                     n.

Nothing to Do With Constipation

stand-up comedy, I couldn't for the life of me
g   agent so that I could audition for television and
commercial roles. Some came as close as being very
interested; no one signed me. I landed a starring role in a
Sleep Country Canada spot because I knew someone who
knew someone. Alas, it never aired. Even though I had the
experience and credentials to warrant an agent, they never
let poor Susan join in any reindeer games.

I now see that I didn't get an agent because I wasn't
supposed to. The universe rocked out another kind of
magic, the non-event. I was being blocked because I

wasn't meant to do stand-up and be in "show biz" for the long haul. Not getting an agent was part of the cosmic nudge that nudged me out of stand-up comedy into a Human Resources career that led me to do the writing and speaking I now do today.

Seeing the non-events in our lives from a higher perspective helps keep one calm and hopeful when stressful thoughts can easily be created. When something we want to have happen doesn't end up happening, that's a sign indicating that the universe has other plans for us. When we don't get the job, when the trip gets canceled, or they don't accept the offer we put on the house, we can see it as negative or we can see that we're meant to experience something different. Our lives often show us that the non-events are just as magical as the events or in other words, they too happen for a reason. Next time something doesn't work out, go back in time to when you were single, you were dating, you were a player...okay, you were dating. You met someone you really liked. You were a smitten kitten. You started dating. It was hot and heavy. When you got to work in the mornings you were that good kind of tired. Everything was wonderful. Then one day, they dumped your rear end... broke your heart into a million pieces. You were devastated. You stayed in your pajamas for roughly a week and a half. Hygiene wasn't much of a priority for you. Your friends would call, but you didn't want to talk to them because you were afraid

Susan Stewart

they would wreck the vibe of your misery. These were the dark days of the soul. Now, think about all the reasons you are so relieved and happy that you didn't end up spending the rest of your living days with them! There's the magic of being blocked!

When things happen in our lives we often call them miracles. When things don't happen as planned, can you see that for some reason you're being blocked and that the non-events in life are very much miracles too?

Your new lenses are ready for pick-up and they can help you see the lighter side of life without having the ability to laugh things off.

*"Here is a new spiritual practice for you.
Don't take your thoughts too seriously."*
- Eckhart Tolle, Stillness Speaks

Chapter 16

Does This Belief System Make Me Look Fat?

"What you believe has more power than what you dream or wish or hope for. You become what you believe." – Oprah Winfrey

The belief systems we carry around with us stem from the thoughts that we continually create and buy into each time we hear it go by in our heads. One of the ways I've learned to lighten up about life is to constantly examine my belief systems and then edit or delete the ones that aren't working for me. I have found it rather easy to pick out the ones that aren't working for me because each time I hear it go by in my head, I feel about as good as I feel after watching CNN or eating eggs Benedict at a greasy spoon diner.

We all have our own individual belief systems and then there are collective belief systems that arise due to a group or society of people thinking and buying into the same things day in and day out. If our belief systems aren't aligned with the truth that we are all perfect, whole, miraculous beings, that uneasy feeling or bad indigestion tends to set in. When belief systems don't sit well with us, like fear-mongering journalism or hollandaise sauce that's been sitting out for a wee bit too long, it's usually because

185

the thoughts are coming from our ego rather than that core truth in us, which we tend to call our spirit or soul.

Think of the ego like the coach of a prize-fighter. Inside all of our heads we've got this short, old man with a towel wrapped around his neck and a cigar in his mouth muttering things to us like, "*You gotta work harder if you're gonna be something*". "*When are you gonna get it together?*" "*You should know better than that by now!*" All the while our souls are sitting cross-legged on a yoga mat doing a breath meditation whispering, "*Relax, it's all good...you're worthy of love and joy no matter what you have and what you do...can we go out dancing soon?*"

Much like the barrage of messages the boxer is fed, to spur him on to fight the good fight, we often listen to that voice inside our heads that's telling us all kinds of things to make us feel separate from everyone, stay competitive, and be viewed as a "winner". The ego keeps us busy and driven by convincing us that our sense of self is merely based on what we do, what we have, and what others think of us. Our ego constantly urges us to do more and have more because that's the ticket to self-worth. Much like a boxer after a big fight, constantly listening to the demanding and critical voice of our ego leads us to feeling tired and beaten up.

Rather than getting sucked into the illusion of the ego, we have the option to silence its voice and crank up the sound of our soul. That higher voice helps us remember all the love we knew before we attached to any worldly conditioning, expectations, and judgment. Below are some ego-mind belief systems that I see worth challenging. This will not sit well with your ego. When you start choosing self-love and self-acceptance, your ego doesn't like it one bit. Your ego pushes away thoughts about cultivating joy and living authentically, because that stuff doesn't *get you ahead in life.* Let's rock the old ego and take a look at belief systems that don't seem to be working for us and consider some new thoughts that just might make your soul sing...

Belief: I *Should*...

When our identity is attached to our accomplishments, possessions, and how we're viewed by others, we can easily wind up believing that there is a master list of "noble actions" that one must execute in order to attain worthiness and be special. We tend to express this ego-mindset by inserting the word, "should", into many of our sentences before stating the "noble action". *"I should travel more." "I should own property rather than rent." "I should clean this house before I do anything else today." "I should have a nicer car."* Have you ever had a bad case of the *shoulds?* Our ego can also lead us to projecting this belief system of "noble actions" on to others and before you know it, we're *shoulding all* over the people we know and work with! *"You should get out more." "You should apply for that job." "You should join Facebook."* Subscribing to the belief that we and the people around us should be doing certain things in life is a huge illusion created by the ego. Just when you thought there are too many rules in life, we've gone and made up a pretend law-book in our minds!

New Thought: I *choose* to take actions, surround myself with people, and place myself in situations that I feel aligned with. Except for what is stated in the real law books (I really *should not* kill someone), everything else in life is optional. I might *want* to join Facebook, but if I would rather have no idea about what is on my friends' minds today, then that's just fine too.

Belief: Productivity Is a Virtue

As our ego likes to try to have us believe that *we are what we do*, a very common belief system is that we *should* be busy. If the house is clean, the errands are done, and the emails have been sent, then I'm a good person worthy of love. The bumper-sticker that says, "*Jesus is coming, look busy!*" is funny, because it's true – it isn't all that far off to what people would say to each other if word got out that the son of God was dropping by on a certain date. Admittedly, in the past, I have chosen to do laundry over going out to see a movie with friends, so I can escape the wrath of that little cigar-smoking man saying, "*There you go being lazy again – good people get jobs done first and only relax if there's time left over.*" It's damn frustrating when you finally do make time to relax or have fun and then you spend the whole time *shoulding* yourself because you feel guilty that you're not busy doing something productive.

The belief that productivity is a virtue runs rampant in today's society. Often when you ask someone how they're doing, they let out a big sigh and say, "*Busy.*" I get the

Susan Stewart

feeling that being busy has become a bit of a competition amongst us humans. Who's the busiest of them all? When your friends tell you how busy they are, have you ever felt bad because you're not as busy as they are? The belief system that productivity is a virtue needs to be challenged because there are too many people who feel down right dirty meeting a friend for lunch on a Saturday afternoon because they feel they would be better people if they were at home washing windows and cleaning the inside of the fridge.

Why are we so busy? The question is, "Why are we so busy?" In addition to it being on that imaginary list of *shoulds*, here's some other list of reasons I have come up with…

- If we aren't busy, we fear that others will think we're lazy (*most of the time people are too busy and too busy thinking about themselves to give our pace of life a second thought*)

- By being busy, we get to avoid the anxiety and guilt that comes over us when we relax (*it's like wearing the same old clothes that you're tired of just to avoid shoppers remorse*)

- Being busy has become a status symbol (*do you ever get the feeling that some people are busy because they want to show off?*)

- We don't know how not to be busy (*and we're too busy to figure it out.*)

189

- Hey, everybody else is busy (*it's like the peer pressure to wear Ralph Lauren button-downs, Bass penny loafers, and acid wash jeans all over again...sigh...*)

New Thought: Being busy is nothing more than being busy. Being busy is not a virtuous act like being honest or being generous. Being busy doesn't create self-worth; however, it can create fatigue that can compromise the quality of our lives. It's a real bummer when you finally make it to the end of a busy week – it's Friday night – and there you are at home fast asleep on the couch by nine o'clock. That's sexy. Having a balance between doing and being can only exist in our lives when we have a loving, supportive voice within ourselves that allows us joy. As the CEO of Yahoo, Carol Bartz, once said at Maria Shriver's annual women's conference, *"Let's be very clear – the issue isn't about balance, it's guilt."* It's time to silence the ego's voice that has made us think that relaxing or having fun is like lying and telling those kids with those UNICEF boxes at Hallowe'en to buzz off because we're keeping our pennies for ourselves, damn it.

"There is only one success – to be able to spend your life in your own way." – Christopher Morley

Belief: I Don't Have Enough

Somewhere along the way a collective hunch was formed to determine whether or not someone has enough in order to be living the "good life". If you take a close look at what is motivating people to live to work, so they can get ahead, it's because the so-called good life is equivalent to earning a certain level of income, owning a house, owning at least one car, going on vacations, wearing certain brands of clothing, and owning every bloody toy that Apple sells. The high standards we create for ourselves and then strive to meet starts by listening to and believing that little, cigar-smoking man in our head telling us that *we are what we have*. For some people, the struggle to have more works for them, but for so many, it's not aligned with their truth. Trying to attain this uniform definition of success is sending many people to the fridge, the bar, the doctor, or the therapist; because the truth is that each and every one of us is unique. It's time to challenge the belief that success is only determined by what you've done and what you've got. What about success being about living the life of *your* dreams? Some folks really want to do what it takes to get the big house, the fancy car, the trips, and all the other bells and whistles. Along with that group of people, there is another group of people who wish they didn't have to work so hard to keep up with the newest version of what's considered to be enough. Subscribing to someone else's version of enough can rob you of the life you truly want just so you too can sing the praises of your PVR, GPS and favourite iPod apps when you attend social events. If you are authentic in your desires to own many possessions that's one thing, but what if the truth is that you would really like to take that money you spend on stuff and use it for something else entirely? What if the truth is that you don't want all this stuff and not buying it would allow you the freedom to make a much-wanted change in your life or career? What if the truth was you would like to yell, "*Screw this stuff, I'm going to go sell seashells by the seashore!*"

New Thought: What's enough *for me*? When we answer that question rather than subscribing to a collective belief system, we often can see how buying into someone else's version of success has driven us to working ten-hour days, answering emails at 11:00 p.m., and bringing our laptops home on weekends.

Belief: Failure Is the Eighth Deadly Sin

I shall explore this belief system through the telling of a story. In the rookie phase of my speaking career, I was booked to deliver an early morning keynote speech at a conference in Niagara Falls. As I arrived in the dark, massive hotel ballroom, I noticed that a trade show was happening on one side of the room and the stage with all the tables for the audience was on the other side of the room. There was no divider in the middle of the room to keep these very separate things separate. I introduced myself to the A/V guy (always my new best friend at events), to get my technical preparation for the presentation rolling. On that particular day, I happened upon an A/V technician who knew nothing about the second largest computer company in the world. This guy didn't know the first thing about Apple products and how to connect my MacBook Pro to the projection system. After about a half hour, we still weren't seeing my slides appear on the big screen behind the stage. After madly scribbling out my notes in preparation to do my speech sans visuals, the A/V guy managed to solve the problem in the eleventh and a half hour. As I looked up and saw my company logo beaming brightly on the screen, my mind started spinning with one side of it happy to be reunited with the original plan and the other half melting down because it was ready to rock it old school with a mic and a dream. Two minutes before I was to deliver my speech and I was struggling to remember my name. I was welcomed on to the stage and as I looked out into the dark abyss, I immediately could tell the energy level in the room was pretty close to what one would experience while delivering a eulogy at a funeral. As I was talking, people in the audience expressed their lack of attention and enthusiasm in different ways. There were some folks chatting with each other, some folks were reading the morning paper, and some just decided to get up and leave. I wasn't mad at the people leaving, by the way – it was more of an overwhelming sense of jealousy. I'd be lying if I said going down those falls in a barrel didn't seem more appealing than what I was up to at the moment. I bombed. I had failed. I had hired professional videographers to come to the event and record all the magic, so it was an expensive failure to boot. Awesome. Because our ego is happiest when others think we're fabulous, taking on the common belief about failure would have led me to view that less than stellar gig as one big screw up and the last thing my young speaking career needed.

New Thought: To fail is to simply arrive at a big sign directing you to go a different way – a way that will serve you better and help you serve others in a more powerful way. Our failures are stepping-stones that lead us to where we can shine our brightest and feel our best. Here are the two main messages written on the sign I saw in Niagara Falls:

1. "Susan, discuss the environment of the venue with your clients so you aren't up on stage competing with a trade show trying to entertain and inspire a bunch of people in a gigantic, dark room."

2. "Susan, be prepared to do your speech without your slides – if the technology works, bonus!"

See the lighter side of screw-ups by contemplating the new direction you want to take based on the experience you were given. After my bomb in Niagara Falls, I skipped the barrel jump down the falls and went on to know a whole lot more about how to set myself and the audience up for success before I take the stage.

Susan Stewart

Create belief systems for yourself by seeing the ego for what it is. The objective is not to abolish the ego completely, but rather, to be aware of the illusion it creates and what it leads you to believe.

Once you are more aware of the ego and the beliefs that aren't working for you, turn your attention to that higher voice inside of you that wants you to be peaceful, feel unconditionally loved, experience joy, and shine that light of yours where ever you go.

Susan Stewart

More Books with Our Authors

Judy Suke
Master of Ceremonies
Big Ideas for the Big Stage
Playing with the Audience
Expert Women Who Speak – Speak Out Vol. 3
Becoming A Professional Speaker
(Coming Soon) *Life Can Be Funny*

Meg Soper
Expert Women Who Speak – Speak Out Vol. 6

Susan Stewart
Awakening the Workplace Vol. 3
Bushido Business
The Mastermind Group- The Power of Mentorship

A Note from Authors

We need your stories. We are working on several books…

Send us your story. We will edit it and check back with you before using it. You can allow us to print your name or be 'the woman from Hamilton', or Anonymous.

Judy Suke:
Life Can Be Funny – Tips to get Through It
Life Can Be Funny in Sales
Life Can Be Funny as a Teacher
Life Can Be Funny as a Policeman
Life Can Be Funny at the Hospital
                    -You get the idea…
Send it to judysuke@bell.net

Meg Soper:
Making a Difference – Stories from the Front Line of Life
Looking for your stories about life – long or short, funny or sad, personal or work-related, inspirational or challenging!
Send it to meg@megsoper.com

Judy Croon:
The Bully Blotter: Are you being bullied at school or work?
Do you have a story or a question to share? (Don't worry, all names will be protected.)
            Send it to judy@JudyCroonSpeaks.com

To order more copies of this book:

From the Stage to the Page
– Life Lessons From Four Funny Ladies

Contact one of the authors …

<u>judysuke@bell.net</u>

<u>meg@megsoper.com</u>

<u>judy@JudyCroonSpeaks.com</u>

<u>susanstewart64@mac.com</u>